# FRAGRANCE AMONG OLD VOLUMES

FROM A PAINTING BY MARGARET ANDERTON

# FRAGRANCE AMONG OLD VOLUMES

## Essays and Idylls of a Book Lover

### By BASIL ANDERTON

B.A. (LOND.), HON. M.A. (DUNELM.)

*WITH ILLUSTRATIONS*

*Essay Index Reprint Series*

*Originally published by:*

KEGAN PAUL, TRENCH, TRÜBNER & CO., LTD.

BOOKS FOR LIBRARIES PRESS, INC.
FREEPORT, NEW YORK

First published 1910
Reprinted 1967

LIBRARY OF CONGRESS CATALOG CARD NUMBER:
67-30171

PRINTED IN THE UNITED STATES OF AMERICA

TO A FEW FRIENDS—

AMONG THEM

THOSE IN ARMSTRONG COLLEGE

NEWCASTLE-UPON-TYNE

# PREFACE

I DESIRE to express my thanks to the Editors of the *Book Lover's Magazine* and of the *Journal of Education* for permission to reprint articles contributed to those periodicals. The Proprietors of the *Book Lover's Magazine*, moreover, were good enough to give me the blocks used to illustrate the articles published by them. I have to thank Miss L. Clay for permission to use her drawing of the Isle of Ulysses. Lastly, I am grateful to my brother, Mr. H. Orsmond Anderton, and to my friend, Professor J. Wight Duff, M.A., D.Litt., for valuable advice on different points.

B. A.

# CONTENTS

# LIST OF ILLUSTRATIONS

x

# I

# MAGLIABECCHI: THE GREAT FLORENTINE BOOKMAN

The spectacle of a life that is a clear-cut unity, and that is spent in the single-minded pursuit of one purpose, as it is rare, so at the least it appeals to our curiosity. It draws us like a work of some great sculptor: even if the subject that is treated have its limitations, we may yet, whilst recognising those limitations, wonder at the sureness and insight with which the work has been brought to its decisive fulfilment.

When we say that a life of this kind has attained its unwonted completeness only by discarding certain elements, which are legitimate and charming enough in themselves, and which form in general no mean part of human life, we are but expressing, after all, a fact which all men, from their own experience, again and again recognise—the restriction of the human powers.

To lament that any great advance in a man's life can be achieved only by narrowing down the range of his work, the object of his desires, is to lament the very constitution of our human nature. More gladly we would laud the clear understanding and resolute strenuousness of those who, seeing where their exceptional powers lie, are content to unfold these powers to their utmost limit, and in high-minded self-denial to forgo other joys.

Thoughts like these are suggested when we endeavour to picture to ourselves the life of such a man as Antonio Magliabecchi—that master-librarian in seventeenth-century Florence. The iron-set face which his portrait presents, the collar with its singular square flap hanging down so loosely, the dingy, threadbare cloak, the long hair tossed and tangled tumultuously over his head — all betoken the romantic story of this man who loved books with a passion that never waned. They bring him in living form before our eyes, till we can verily see the old librarian moving amongst his books, and can watch him as, with a great volume in one arm, he settles himself into his roomy, creaking cane chair, which he has dragged where the light will fall conveniently upon the page. Then he will undo the clasp, and forthwith a strange keenness—wolfishness rather—springs into his eyes ; his lips part, and deep curves form in his cheeks as, in a ravening eagerness, he devours page after page.

Of the earliest days of this great bookman but little is known. According to one account his mother, a widow, had him taught the elements of

Latin and drawing, and apprenticed him to Comparini, a famous Florentine goldsmith. According to others, however, we come across him first, in the Florence of 1645, as a greengrocer's lad, poring over the printed wrappings of his master's parcels. He could not read, the tale runs, but was yet fascinated by the magical outward symbols of learning. Hard by there dwelt a bookseller who observed this, and spoke to the lad. Pleased with the earnestness of his answers, and foreseeing partly whither this passionate love for a dimly descried knowledge might lead, he at last promised, in answer to tearful implorings, to take little Antonio into his own shop (provided his old master could be won over), and there set him to work among his books. The fruit-seller proving not obdurate, Magliabecchi thus at last found the environment and the outlet that his nature craved. How quickly he learnt to read needs not be said. That stage once past, he made swift advance, and as time went on his knowledge of the names, the places on the shelves, and at last of the matter itself of the books, grew steadily, inevitably, till it surpassed even that of his master. He read well-nigh every book that came within his grasp. Rumour of his accurate memory and wondrous diligence began to spread ere long among book-loving Florentines. Ermini, the librarian to the Cardinal de Medicis, heard of him, found means of seeing him, and, struck by his indubitable

power, spoke of him to others and made him
known amongst learned men.  These tried him
from time to time, and could not but marvel to
find how often his advice about authors to be
examined, or his clear knowledge of rarer books
to be seen, proved valuable.  In the very letters
of his name (Latinised as Antonius Magliabechius)
Father Angelo Finardi saw the almost perfect
anagram *Is unus bibliotheca magna : He is in
himself a great library.*  So it was that as years
went on Magliabecchi's fame reached the ears of
the Grand Duke himself, Cosmo III. ; who, being
an ever watchful patron of such men, kept eye
upon the learned bookman, and in 1673 put him
in charge of the library he had lately established
in his palace.

Magliabecchi was by this forty years of age.
Half his life was done, and the remaining half,
which was that of his wider fame, had now to be
lived.  With hardly a break he lived it in that
library.  Of the rooms provided for him in the
palace he would have none, for he abhorred cere-
monial and restraint.  Careless of the outside
world, he resolved to live deeply amidst his books
till he had mastered their secrets and had made
that great library responsive to his every touch,
like some instrument of sweet, vast music.  For
his sleep, when he must needs rest, two cane chairs
would suffice.  Three eggs boiled hard would
appease his hunger, and a draught of cold water,

or may be a little good wine, quench his thirst.
Did he want physic? Treacle suited him well,
and was readily got. Of tobacco, which should
clear his mind and, when melancholy, soothe him,
he would ever have ample store within reach. In
bringing this his new toil to its great accomplish-
ment, he would make laboriousness his dear com-
rade, temperate living his firm ally, tobacco his
counsellor. And thus armed he would do battle
with the dwellers in this silent realm on which he
was entered, till he had forcefully made them
meek vassals under his proud yet reverent kingship. With a clear, unerring certainty he would
know what was the scope and power of each book,
in which alcove was its dwelling-place, on which
very shelf. Nay, more; his fame should stretch
beyond his own borders, till even the books in
distant lands should learn somewhat of his gover-
nance. Catalogues should discover to him their
whereabouts; learned men, under ruthless ques-
tioning, should tell him which were of rarer breed
and power; librarians, under his written bidding,
should reveal whether they might not be bought
over into his service, and at what price.

Was this ambition very proud? Was it fore-
doomed, think you, even when books in that
seventeenth century were less plenty than in these
days, to overleap itself? Yet perchance there
were 'giants in the earth' still. And, indeed,
who, seeing his picture—looking into those unrest-

ing, insatiate eyes, and observing that tameless
mouth and jaw—or is not even that disregarded
dress significant, unrenewed for many a year
whilst his purpose was yet in process of fulfilling?
—who, seeing these things, should doubt that in
the end he accomplished all his will?

And what he acquired in this slow strenuousness, he imparted in a regal profusion. The
Florentine scholar, busied with Aristotle and the
schoolmen, won from him easeful guidance to
some unremembered volume. The priest, fain to
write the miracles of his loved patron saint, heard
from Magliabecchi of the hundred authors who,
in set treatise or in passing observation, had told
already of his wondrous deeds. To all that came
—and they were many, both from far and near—
did he give rich gifts from the storehouse of his
memory. They must come to him; for he himself went not abroad save perchance a few miles
out of Florence to see some precious book or rare
manuscript. They must come to him; for he
would be a little proud, and say that his kingship
merited that homage. But being come, they
should be regally entertained. Thus he lived,
whilst year by year old age was coming upon
him. His friends loved him well, and his foes—
for how should so strong a man escape, or greatly
care to escape, all enmity?—found him, from the
resourceful subtlety of his learning, grimly for-
midable. Nay, even the Pope himself would fain

have enlisted Magliabecchi's powers on his side. He, however, prized not the fighting of other men's battles, nor the scattering their foes like chaff. More fain was he to abide there in peace, doing his own work amongst his books. Sweeter by far to read through the long, silent night, till with the ruddy sunrise he welcomed the familiar ray that fell aslant on a row of vellum-covered books, tinging them with a rarer glory that befitted well the spirit of his domain—the spirit of peaceful yet scholarly seclusion, of clear yet manifold erudition. And if at the last his bodily powers began to wane, well, perchance he would take his sleep henceforth in more comfort, lying in some wooden-framed hammock slung between two bookshelves. If teeth must needs drop out, why, he must munch the softer bread. The joys of tobacco waned not, at least; rather did they wax greater.

Thus husbanding his strength, he would still learn many a strange secret of hidden lore, and would still add to his master's library many a priceless treasure. His own books, too, of which —thanks to the rich gifts of Florentines—he had now gathered many and many a hundred, should reach the full tale of thirty thousand; and these he would, in a last generosity, bequeath for ever to his loved city of Florence.

In all these things did Magliabecchi accomplish the hopes that he had formed and the thought that was in his mind.  Page after page of his life did  he turn, ever according  to  his will.   And at last, when all was done, Death himself turned the final page for him as  he  lay a-reading  one night in  his  cane  chair.    And  in  the  morning  they found him lying there in peace.

## II

## THE BEQUEST: A MS. 'BOOK OF WISDOM'

> '. . . Ingenuas didicisse fideliter artes
> Emollunt mores, nec sinuisse feros.'

So our worthy friend and 'peccable Latinist' Colonel Newcome! In the latter half of the sixteenth century there was living in Holland a certain William Diert, whom we may conjecture to have been in some ways a counterpart to Thackeray's hero, yet who had read more widely in Latin, possibly also in Greek. He had passed his life in troublous times, and his love for the *literæ humaniores*, though genuine and earnest, had not had opportunity for high training. He had, we gather, been obliged to take his part in what Motley calls 'the great agony through which the Republic of Holland was ushered into life,' and, probably in his case through strenuous fighting, accurate scholarship had been hard to attain, harder to maintain. He had studied for a time at Cologne, and as the end of his life came near looked back through a vista of 'foul

9

and turbulent wars' to those pleasant student days. This love for his early studies, together with another interest—his love for his son William —was the great concern of his failing energies, and he longed, as Thackeray's hero longed, to see this son grow into a wise and steadfast man, free from prejudice and firmly established in virtue. For a long time he pondered how he should compass his desire; and at the last this seemed best to him. He would gather together the mottoes and old words of wisdom which had guided himself in the ways of his life, and would write them out with his own hand, making, as it were, a little 'Book of Wisdom.' They should be, moreover, all in Latin—that tongue which had so lasting a fascination for him—to the end that young William might be drawn, as by spells of art, to give heed to the counsels he offered. And this book he would bequeath to him, placing it in the same chest with his other riches—riches less enduring if more costly.

So he chose a little book, vellum bound, and tied with green tapes, and with a border stamped round each page. On the second page he wrote out the *index argumentorum*, meaning to divide his book into nine parts, as follows :

'The wise man alone lives well. (Sapiens solus bene vivit.)

The wise man is the true worshipper of God. (Sapiens verus dei cultor.)

The wise man searcheth not into the mysteries
   of God.  (Sapiens arcana dei non scrutatur.)
The wise man seeketh true riches.  (Sapiens
   veras querit opes.)
The wise man is truly noble.  (Sapiens vere
   nobilis.)
The wise man considers what the tongue
   brings to pass.  (Sapiens quid lingua
   efficiat considerat.)
The wise man ruleth his passions.  (Sapiens
   affectibus suis imperat.)
The wise man feareth not death.   (Sapiens
   mortem non timet.)
How wisdom is gained.  (Sapientia quomodo
   acquiratur.)'
On the third page he begins a preface or letter
to his son, to this effect :—

### ' *William Diert to his son William*

' Even as without learning (the philosophers
say) life is, as it were, the image of death, so
without some mode of right living life is not life,
but the counterfeit of death.   For this cause,
dear William, I thought it well to leave you this
book as a remembrance of me, for in it you can
see, pointed out as it were with a finger, the way
of living well and happily ; and you may easily
observe that the right mode of living has been so
praised and approved by all the wise, whether
Gentile or Christian, that they have thought an

upright, temperate, and good life better than erudition. The good life, as they say, has beauty even without learning, but learning without such life is detestable ; the man, however, to whose lot both fall would be felt by all to be truly happy. You should ever regard the thought and judgments of men more than the men themselves. For human feeling, planted in us by Nature herself, makes us love and care for some more than others, and, on the other hand, reject and abuse some ; and hence judgments and sayings are more or less valued according as their author charms or displeases us. For this cause you will not much heed whether he be Gentile or Christian, but will rather consider the good and prudent judgments that he hath made : since a healthful judgment is not to be despised because its author is humble, nor is it the man who speaks that we should regard, but what is spoken. Perchance you will find some mistakes in grammar, since I have not studied Latin except in so far as, at the time of Holland's foul and turbulent wars, I gathered these sayings together out of various authors, for my exercise at Cologne. Do you therefore, if there is any error, correct it, but, above all, guide your mind and life by the instruction of these sayings, and see to it that to these perishable and frail possessions you join also those riches which in shipwreck can swim off with their master, upon which fortune hath no

power, and which follow their owner when he
fareth away hence. Farewell.

'COLOGNE, *February* 15, 15

[*Guilielmus Diert, Guilielmo suo*

Quemadmodvm sine doctrina (ut aiunt philo-
sophi) vita est quasi mortis imago, ita absque
ratione bene viuendi vita non est vita, sed simul-
achrum mortis. Propterea mi Guilielme con-
sultum fore duxi, ut libellum hunc pro mei
monumento tibi relinquerem. In hoc enim licet
videas viam quasi digito commonstratam bene,
ac beate viuendi, facileque perspicias rectam
vivendi rationem, omnibus sapientibus, tam gen-
tilibus, quam christianis semper laudatam, pro-
batam que adeo fuisse, ut probam, modestam,
bonamque vitam meliorem eruditione esse exis-
timarint. Nam uti inquiunt bona vita, sine
doctrina, gratiam habet, at doctrina, sine vita
detestabilis est. Cui autem utrumque contingit,
hunc certe beatum esse cui libet constare potest.
Semper magis debes respicere sententias, quam
autores, eo quod humano affectu, nobis a natura
insito, unum magis diligamus, ac colamus altero,
et econtra alium reiiciamus, ac vituperamus,
atque inde sententiae, dictaue plus minus aesti-
mantur, prout ipse autor nobis arrideat aut
displiceat. Proinde non curabis fueritne gentilis,
an christianus, sed id quod bene, prudenterquæ

sensit, quia propter autoris humilitatem, non est contemnenda salubris sententia, nec spectandum est quis dicat, sed quid dicatur. Fortassis quaedam grammatices vitia invenies, cum latinitati non studuerim, preterquam quod, foedissimis turbulentissimisque Hollandiae bellis, Coloniae, exercitii gratia, has sententias ex variis autoribus collegerim. Tu igitur si quid sit vitii corrige, sed praecipue mentem ac vitam juxta horum dictorum institutum dirige, et fac ut hisce caducis ac fragilibus bonis, eas quoque adiungas opes, quae nauifracta simul cum domino enatent, et in quas nullum ius habet fortuna, quaeque sequuntur herum suum hinc emigrantem. Vale: Coloniae, 15 calendarum Martii, A° 1577.]

This letter is finished on the fifth page, and on the sixth he starts, without further let or hindrance, upon the counsels themselves. After what he has here said, one is prepared to face with tolerance, and even with respect, a few unwonted forms in Latin words (*e.g.*, 'respundit'), and here and there some strange grammar (*e.g.*, 'Deus magis spectat affectus immolantium quam victima ; or, again, 'Deus detestatur os bilingua'). With Diert, as with many another man, what he aimed at was higher than what he completely achieved. It is already much that in so restless an age he did not abandon his love for tranquil and high pursuits, nor desist from his quest after knowledge. If in the midst of wars

and rumours of wars he had learnt to possess his
soul in peace, and to breathe an air that was free
from turmoil, from prejudice, and from vanity, it
seems no great matter though his speech exhibit
some solecisms, or though his way of thinking
be at times discursive and somewhat irrelevant.
Since he loved learning much, not a little should
be forgiven this Stoic-Christian warrior.

In some instances curious spelling, such as
'tollorare' and 'temporare,' might be explained
partly by the scarcity of books for one busily
engaged in wars, and a consequent difficulty in
holding the true form of words in accurate
remembrance ; partly by supposing him, during
the unsettled times through which he had passed,
to have talked and heard more Latin than he
read, for that would be the obvious way, in an
age when Latin was a more general tongue than
now, of retaining some grasp upon the language.

The upright manuscript itself is in many
places most graceful and symmetrical, though
here and there the letters slope over falteringly to
the right, and the lines become curved instead of
straight — perhaps, on one day and another,
through failing vitality, or through the throbbing of
some old wound.  He prints each letter separately,
with one or two exceptions ; thus the s and t are
cunningly united, sometimes with one curve, sometimes with two.  In the n's and u's the down
strokes have the connecting line indifferently

at the top or bottom, though to avoid confusion a little curl, similar to that used in German manuscript (the so-called U-Bogen), is placed over every *u*. Final *m*'s are often indicated simply by a small stroke, straight or curved, above the line ; *ij* and *ii* are run into a *y*, with a dot over each part of the fork. The enclitic *-que* is often written with an *æ* (diphthong), though this is sometimes corrected ; it is also frequently abbreviated to a *q* and a little flourish. Stops, which now and then are needlessly abundant, are for the most part absent, even to obscurity. The ink used was excellent, and is now blacker, after more than three hundred and thirty years, than many a modern ink after a single year.

The loving care which he gave to his work may be seen, apart from the general beauty of the writing, in the neat erasures with which he often sets a slip right, and perhaps in the cutting out of two pages, probably marred by some accident or blots. The quaint little flourishes which spring up here and there, as it were spontaneously, tell the same tale.

With these as some of the minor characteristics of his work, Diert entered upon his *Sententiæ ad Bene Vivendi Rationem Pertinentes et Solum Sapientem Bene Vivere Declarantes*. The first part is to show, as has been said, that 'The wise man alone lives well (Sapiens solus bene vivit),' and he establishes the truth of his text in about one hundred and twenty extracts, all in Latin, from many sources.  He starts with the (partial) quotation from Proverbs : ' Wisdom is the one way of living well and rightly ; her ways are ways of pleasantness, and all her paths are peace ' ('Sapientia unica est via bene recteque vivendi viæ eius viæ pulchræ et omnes semitæ eius rectæ et pacificæ sunt ') ; and he goes on to draw wisdom from many wells, some deeper, and some shallower.  Those which he uses most frequently are the Bible (including the Apocrypha), Cicero, and Erasmus.  The following, however, also appear, more or less often, though always in a Latin guise :—

| | | |
|---|---|---|
| Arcesilas. | Horatius. | Plato. |
| Cato. | Iamblichus. | Plutarch. |
| Cheremonis. | Isocrates. | Seneca. |
| Chilo. | Lactantius. | Simonides. |
| Democrites. | Lycurgus. | Socrates. |
| Diogenes. | Menander. | Solon. |
| Epictetus. | Phocion. | Taule. |
| An Epicurean. | Phocyladis. | Terence. |
| Epicurus. | Pita, ⎫ (? Pythagoras.) | Theofrastus. |
| Euripedes. | Pitago. ⎭ | Zeno. |

The spelling is, of course, Diert's own.

It is a curious list, and some of the names are not easily intelligible.  One is driven to doubt whether Diert's work on these authors had in every case been at first hand, or whether he had in some part had his way smoothed by a previous

B

(and rather slipshod) collector of aphorisms. He may, too, be trying at times to record the quotations employed by certain preachers of his day. If his reading had really been so wide and varied, such constructions as the following are the more casual and strange : 'Indecora sapienti vox non putaram aut non expectaram.' 'Ita illius [scil. Pori] oratine [*sic*] submovit regem [scil. Alexandrum] ut modeste sua fortuna uteretur memor ipsi posse accidere quo acciderat Poro.' However, these are quite exceptionally weak, and the question as to the particular degree of Diert's scholarship need not have undue prominence. It is his general character that is chiefly of interest.

While, of course, it would take far too long to translate the whole of his little book, we shall, by considering some of his more typical *sententiæ* (many of which possess intrinsic interest), find some of the evidence for our conclusions about the man himself who gathered these counsels together. Let us turn once more, then, to what he has to say on his first thesis, that 'the wise man alone lives well.'

'If thou seek wealth, what has silver richer than wisdom? . . . if victory, she is better than warlike arms ; if power, she is of all things the most powerful ; if eloquence, she giveth skill to the tongues of children ; if life, she inspireth her sons ; if sweet pleasure, there is no bitterness in her intercourse, but rather joy and gladness; if a kingdom, love wisdom, and thou shalt bear rule for ever.'

'Wisdom alone hath taught us, along with all things else, that one hardest thing—to know ourselves.'

'There are two gifts of wisdom: the contempt of death, and of pain.'

'A wise man changeth his plans after the order of the times; but to be changeful without cause is the defect of the fickle.'

'Cato used to say that fools are of more service to the wise than the wise to fools; because the wise readily see the mistakes of fools and avoid them, but with the fools it is not so.'

'Wisdom alone of all things is immortal.'

'All remedy for our faults and offences must be sought from philosophy.'

'No deity is absent when prudence is present.'

'Nothing is quieter than wisdom; nothing more turbulent than vice.'

'One said to Diogenes, "I am not fitted for philosophy." "Why, then," he answered, "dost thou live, if thou hast no care for living aright? For man liveth not merely that he may live, but that he may learn to live aright."'

'As in a fountain there never faileth water bubbling out therefrom, so in a wise man joy is ever present, even though outward things be changed.'

'It is very ill for a philosopher to teach otherwise than he lives.'

'Nature gives living; philosophy gives living aright.'

'A wise and brave man never groaneth, unless, perchance, when he braceth himself to resoluteness.'

'What is there more incongruous than if one that is a professed grammarian speak barbarously? Or if he that would be reckoned a musician sing strangely out of tune? So a philosopher offending in his mode of life is thereby the worse.'

'The life of the wise seemeth madness to fools.'

'Socrates said, "A wise man should remember the past, should act in the present, should be wary of the future."'

'As those that sail with fair winds hold their ship's tackle in readiness wherewith to guard against an adverse storm, so those who are wise during their good fortune prepare and dispose their minds even to misfortunes.'

'A prudent man hath small faith in the faithless.'

The next heading that we come to is this: 'The wise man is the true worshipper of God (Sapiens verus dei cultor'). This is not treated at so great length as the preceding, only about fifty-five *sententiæ* being quoted. As his texts, etc., though excellent in themselves, are to a large extent irrelevant, we will be brief.

'The wise man observeth the law after the mind of God, but the fool after the judgment of his own heart.'

'God more regardeth the minds of those that sacrifice than the victim.'

'No place is dearer to God than the heart of man.'

'Better is obedience than the victim of fools.'

The next chapter, showing that 'The wise man searcheth not into the mysteries of God,' is still shorter, and comprises only seventeen quotations.

'Oh, the height of the riches of wisdom and of the knowledge of God! How vast are His judgments, how hidden His paths! Who knoweth the mind of the Lord, or who hath been His counsellor?'

'Seek not the things that are higher than thou art, neither inquire into the things that are mightier than thou; but think ever of those things that God hath taught thee, and be not concerned about many works; for it is not needful for thee to see with thine eyes those things that are hidden.'

'Being mortal, let your care be of things that are mortal.'

' Inquire not what shall become of thee, for God willeth not that thou shouldest know it.'

' Socrates, who was alone judged the wisest of all men, would never argue concerning lofty matters, since they are beyond the reach of men ; and he would say, "What is above us nowise concerns us." '

The next division, ' The wise man seeketh true riches (Sapiens veras querit opes),' is a somewhat longer one, and contains over sixty selections :

' Nature daily admonisheth us how small things she needs, how few, how cheap.'

' Nothing so showeth a narrow and small mind as the loving of riches ; nothing is more honourable and noble than the contemning of wealth.'

' What the crowd prizeth—to wit, riches—that do thou despise ; and what the crowd regardeth not—to wit, uprightness, virtue, and learning— that do thou prize.'

' Furnish thyself with those riches which in shipwreck can swim off with their master.'

' We must think that happiness lies not in the greatness of possessions, but in the wellbeing of the mind ; nor would any man say that the body is in good case because it is clothed in fine raiment, but because it enjoys health and is well ; but where the soul is well ordered, that man is truly rich.'

'When the ambassadors of Philip, King of the Macedonians, offered great gifts to Phocion, and exhorted him to receive them since he was poor, and said, although indeed he could do without them, yet to his children they would be needful, since it would be hard for them in the greatest poverty to attain to the glory of their father; "If," said he, "they are like me, this same plot of ground will nourish them which has raised me to this dignity; if they are unlike, I do not wish that their luxury should be nourished and increased at my cost."'

'A wise man carries all his riches with him.'

'When Demetrius had taken Megara, he called Stilbo, the philosopher, to him, and asked him whether any one of the soldiers had taken away any goods of his. "No one," said he; "for I saw no one that could carry off any wisdom"; recognising that only the goods of the mind were not exposed to the violence of war.'

'It is a great dowry when an uncorrupted character is brought to a marriage; as a Spartan woman, being asked what dowry she would bring to her husband, "Modesty," she answered, "handed down from my fathers."'

'Diogenes was wont to argue that "all things belong to the gods; the wise are the friends of the gods; friends have all things in common; therefore all things belong to the wise."'

The next thesis, that 'The wise man is truly noble,' is disposed of in about two pages. The following may be taken as examples :—

'The nobility of the wise man consists in virtue.'

'It is far better to grow noble than to be born noble.'

'If you would secure glory and honour, be such as you would fain be reputed.'

'An honourable fame is a second patrimony.'

The sixth part of the book (it will be remembered that there were nine divisions in all) is entitled 'The wise man considereth what the tongue bringeth to pass.' It is by far the longest of all, and extends to more than thirty pages.

'He that useth many words hurteth his own soul.'

'The heart of a fool is placed in his mouth, but the mouth of a wise man is placed in his heart.'

'A guileful tongue loveth not truth, and a slippery mouth worketh ruin.'

'He that answereth before he heareth showeth himself to be a fool, and worthy of confusion.'

'Answer a fool after his folly.'

'Answer not a fool after his folly.'

'There is a time when it is meet to answer a fool after his folly, lest he should seem wise unto himself; there is a time when it is not meet to answer a fool after his folly, lest thou shouldest become like him.    Christ heard, "Thou art a Samaritan," and He held His peace ; He heard, "Thou hast a devil," and He gainsaid the injury.'

'If any man thinketh himself to be religious and bridleth not his tongue, his religion is vain.' (This, by the way, is attributed to Erasmus.)

'The tongue of many men outrunneth their minds.'

'It is not always *what* is said or proposed that should be examined, but *with what mind* it is said.'

'In speaking, thou must consider not what is pleasant to thee to say, but what will help others, or what is expedient for them to hear.'

'A fool when he holds his tongue nowise differs from a wise man.'

'Athenodorus, the philosopher, warned Augustus, when he was about to depart, to do or say nothing in anger without first saying over the Greek alphabet in its order.    Cæsar, pleased with that counsel, embraced the man, and said, "I have need of you," and kept him with him for a year to learn silence of such a master.'

'A word once uttered cannot be recalled, but thought can be corrected.'

'Talkativeness has always been joined with folly, and eloquence with wisdom.'

'The ill that is wrought by silence can be [set

right] by speech; but a word, when once uttered, flies far away beyond our recall.' (The Latin is as follows: 'Quod silentio peccatum est potest recerciri [*sic*] silentio: Sed semel emissum volat irrevocabile verbum.' Though this second line is a hexameter of Horace's, the *sententia* is given as that of Simonides.)

''Twas pithily said by one, that "For speech we have men as masters; for silence, the gods."'

'A weapon, when hurled, falleth not back on him that sent it, but rather bringeth destruction upon others; but a word, when uttered, bringeth destruction upon no man more surely than upon him that sent it forth.'

'No thanks are due to a prodigal who bestows, not through kindness, but through a diseased mind; so the faith of keeping silence is not due to him who was the first to break the covenant of silence.'

'They who have the falling sickness fall not where they will, but wheresoever the sickness hath seized them; so they that have the disease of the tongue slip and fall alike in the greatest things and in the least.'

'No man speaketh aright but he that hath first learnt to hold his peace.'

'Nature hath given to man one mouth and two ears, that we may hear more than we speak.'

'Who would not shudder if one offered him

wine mixed with poison? Yet that poison is more hurtful which a flatterer or a backbiter offereth thee, since thou drinkest it in through greedy ears.'

'It is cowardly to assail those with thy tongue who cannot answer thee.'

'A slanderer often re- . . .'

Diert's work of love got no further. At the end of a page, and in the middle of a word, just where he should have turned the leaf, the writing ceases. Latterly the writing had grown less symmetrical, less accurate; his powers seem to have been ebbing, and at last the final summons came. He must leave his willing toil, and must go without even setting hand to the three outstanding parts of his little book. The arguments thus left untouched were: 'The wise man ruleth his passions,' 'The wise man feareth not death,' and 'How wisdom is gained.' But it may well be that the old man's sudden silence spoke more intimately to the son than many quotations could have done.

Of the son we know nothing. Here and there in the manuscript we find an alteration which might suggest that he had begun, as his father bade him in the letter prefixed to the book, to correct some mistakes ('grammatices vitia'), for the hand seems different. But such marks are few and far between, and we cannot from such small tokens know what manner of man he was that made them, nor how he used this bequest of his father's. To call his spirit from 'the vasty deep' by virtue of symbols so imperfect is beyond the reach of our slight arts of magic. Nor can we tell what has been, during the last three centuries and more, the history of the little volume itself. Into whose hands has it fallen during its wanderings? How have its owners regarded it? All that is sure is this: some years ago it reached a second-hand book shop in the north of England, and, being there found by the present writer, passed into his possession.

## III

## FRAGRANCE AMONG OLD BOOKS

In one alcove of a certain library there seemeth
ever to linger the scent of tea-roses. Two
maiden ladies are wont to read there, mostly on
Saturday afternoons, and once they were wearing
each a sweet cluster of these flowers. Perchance
some rarer balminess of air and sunshine had
cleared their vision and compelled the unwonted
purchase; for they never wore them before nor
after—nor, indeed, any flowers at all. They live
in the town, and have no fragrant garden where
sun-lit flowers thrive ; they are poor in this
world's goods, so perforce they cannot buy.
Therefore we see them clad ever soberly in close-
fitting bonnets that, through some obscure tinge
of colour, are just not black, and, if the weather
is cold, in some quaint cape and woollen gloves.
Their skirts are short for the cleaner walking ;
their boots stout and, it may be, patched ; their
hair smoothly braided.

In such guise are these sisters, Miss Joan and

Miss Dorothy, wont to come on Saturdays to their corner of the library, and to gather the substance of some lesson that they must give to their scholars next week; for they are school-mistresses. In *Chambers's Encyclopædia* they find great store of wealth, and ply their pencils and little note-books, whispering and nodding to one another. Or the librarian, seeing that they are perchance busied about the early explorers, may show them, in an old volume of travels, some strange tale of marvels in newly-discovered lands. With what rapt wonder do they read, with what whispered exclamations of awe and delight. But at last—well, 'tis hard in these voyages to sever fact from fancy—how shall they be sure which is which? How terrible if they made a mistake in class! So they turn once more to the *terra firma* of *Chambers's Encyclopædia*, though Miss Dorothy, the younger, whose face has still hints of comeliness, heaves a little sigh at abandoning those bold sailors, and the rush o' the sea, and that free, strong life. But she defers happily to her wiser sister, gladdened at heart for this glimpse into a bygone wonderland; and presently, their work done, they will get up, still nodding and smiling, and go home armed at all points for the lesson to their highest class—which consists of two big girls.

Teaching does not bring them riches; but if they know that they are poor, the knowledge

afflicts them not.  They work on with a happy
naturalness, now and again going, note-book still
in hand (for they have ever an afterthought for
their school), to some free lecture in the town.
One thing only about their school-work troubles
them — and it is that they can spare so few
pounds a term as salary to the teacher who helps
them.    Still, the teacher is generally loth to leave
them, and grows to love them not a little.

For gifts of charity they have but scanty pence.
Therefore, that they be not found at the last
empty-handed, they give of their toil ; and on
Sunday, after their week's teaching, will don a
somewhat wider lace-collar, and plod down twice
a day to the Church rooms, in fair weather or
foul, to teach once more in the Sunday School.
Ye sweet-minded women !   Small wonder if after
this labour your faces look at times pale and
pinched, and your eyes too alert and hungry.

But if we would see them in a glow of hospit-
able happiness, we must call upon them in their
home, and have a cup of tea with them.   The
tea-pot is ready to their hand, and while Miss
Dorothy cuts into a little cake (kept in readiness
for visitors, and only eaten privately when quite
stale), Miss Joan brews the tea.

So they spend their life—a life that, if simple-
minded, hath yet a certain dignity and recol-
lectedness ; if austere towards themselves, is yet,
within its means, generous to others ; if labori-

ous, yet taketh delight in the society of friends. And the fragrance of such a life is, one may fancy, not ill symbolised by the flowers they wore on that memorable day.

# IV

## CONCORDIO : THE STORY OF A POOR MUSIC MASTER

An enthusiast who can bear the brunt of poverty for sixty years, and whom no despair of wide recognition can daunt, arrests our attention. Possessed with ideals of teaching his art, and toiling ceaselessly to give these ideals systematic embodiment, he is worthy of study and of no meagre admiration. And if, at the last, tragedy shall touch him with her terrible finger, so that his final act, though perchance mistaken, shall reveal at least a simple manliness and an unselfish strength, our admiration is imbued with something more akin to pity and to love.

In some such epitome might we describe Concordio, a poor music master, whom we first knew halfway through his life. As to his early years, one could gather but little, though gradually it became clear that, a Bohemian by birth, he was early enamoured of music, and resolved at all costs to devote his life to her service. To this end, shunning the imminent military service, which he hated like all else akin to bloodshed, he left his native land and travelled about the Continent, devoting himself with rare singleness to the art he so loved, and gaining his livelihood now in one theatrical band, now in another, as leader of the violins. After some years, he settled in London as a teacher of the violin, viola, 'cello, and piano, as well as of harmony, and before long found himself impelled towards the development of some new system of harmony— that system which was henceforth to be the central object of his life. To this, year after year, he devoted his leisure ; on this he spent the whole balance left from his earnings when his bare subsistence had been paid for. And as the progressing parts of his system got printed, he saw to it that copies were placed in the Library of the British Museum, hoping that recognition of his work's value, lingeringly delayed in the present, might be won in after years, to the lasting benefit of his beloved art. And should his life be even ended before the recognition came, well, he would regard the copies in the Museum as a bequest to the nation which had, after all, enabled him to live his life and do his work.

For the sake, then, of this work he sacrificed many a thing that would have given him the keenest joy. Despite his love for animals, he would keep no living things near him — no

canary even—fearing lest he should spend too
much time at its cage, or should not be resolute
to stop its singing when work was to be done.
This world's pleasure, as such, he did not seek.
True, composition was a pleasure ; but when
composing he was, as he once said, not in this
world. Holidays he took rarely and briefly, and,
as it were, at haphazard ; for he would start
from his lodgings with a bag (in which inevitably
was his manuscript), and inquiring, at some
chance railway terminus, to which seaside village
the next train went, would journey thither,
staying for a week or so—changing, indeed, his
London surroundings and air, but never relaxing
from his task. When in London itself, his
recreation was of the simplest. A walk by the
river Lea (prettier by far in the bygone days)
would on Fridays, when he was in the neighbourhood, be a refreshment to him—that, and always
tobacco. Or on Sundays he might, now and
once again, go for a few hours to Croydon, where
also he had friends to welcome his rare visits.

Yet with this rigour of strenuous toil, his
gentleness with children was conspicuous. His
quaint inventions to win their interest and beguile
music's 'long art' will be remembered. The dots
which signify repetition became with him 'two
little policemen who send you back to the beginning before they let you pass.' Did you, even at
a third hearing of the piece you were learning,

still make mistakes, and begin to grow dis-
couraged? Though he would not indeed tick
the piece as known, yet he would half persuade
you that it was he who, in the accompaniment,
had made a slip, and not you in your part; and
so would have it again next week. And at his
going you would warn him to be sure and know
it next time. His liking for such inversions
would often re-appear, too, in his talk with
children over a cup of tea. In his view, it was
the early worm that got picked up by the bird.
The rose would, by any other name, be as prickly.
To make a gun, again, you take a hole and put a
steel barrel round it. Or if a riveted jug caught
his eye, he would become at once interested—
'Ah, curious! The stitches are all on one side.'

In his more difficult work of conducting his
suburban quintet classes, he was strenuous and
alert. He led the violins. A little man, with
black bushy round beard and whiskers, and
gleaming gold-rimmed spectacles, he sat there in
frock coat and speckled brown trousers—invariably turned up, and whole inches too short. As
he played he would shout a restraining 'one, two,
three,' to hurrying flutists (who, in easy parts,
went apace); or would recall strayed 'cellists by
stamping with his foot at the beginning of each
bar; or would set painful second fiddles right by
playing a bar or two of their parts (for he knew
these symphonies by heart). Or, if on all sides

the error became inextricable, he would tap the
stand with his bow, or even, in case of direst
wholesale uproar, rap the resounding back of his
fiddle; and, when he had won silence, would say,
'Ah, I think we go back to the double bar.'
And so at length they would win through the
symphony, when he, good man, could mop his
brow after the toilsome leadership; and during
the last ten minutes or so they would try some
gavotte or waltz, or an easy overture.  And, the
two hours being done, he would rise, and with a
'Thank you, gentlemen,' would put away his
violin.    Then  he  would  perhaps  come  in  to
supper, and quickly recover his serenity, saying
with a swift twinkle of his spectacled blue eyes,
'Ah, that glass of beer have saved my life!'  So
he  would  become  'his  own  man'  again,  and
would sit chatting at his ease for a while over
frugal fare, till presently he would pull out his
watch, look at it, and, invariably saying, 'Ah, I
just catch my train,' would leave ere his welcome
had had a chance of being outstayed.

With such sane vigour and patience he would
teach his class, training them until they were at
last fairly well in hand.  And if their performance
never attained brilliancy, yet those who worked
there caught many an echo at least, in their way
through forty or fifty symphonies, of sweet
harmonies whose memory might abide with them.

Year after year, now in one part of London,

now in another, such work went on, till he was well past middle age ; and his friends wondered how lightly his years sat upon him.

Of his powers as a soloist on the violin one would not, at least in these later years, say a great deal. Teaching was his great work, performing secondary. To hear him play his ' Sehnsucht,' however, was to get some illumination on the more pathetic side of his nature. It was written, as one might conceive, in the early days of his struggling with the world, when once, under a stress of work, and perhaps after some heavy disappointment, his thoughts reverted longingly, almost hysterically, to the peace of his childhood's home far away. The old man would still play it to us from time to time.

By now he was well forward with his 'system,' and was printing the later parts. Busily he still toiled at it, describing it once quaintly as the 'result of thirty years' imprisonment with hard labour.' When reviews of it, or indeed of any of his compositions, appeared in the papers, he would cut them out and gather them together ; showing them, with ruthless honesty, in such fashion that the unfavourable notices could be seen side by side with the favourable.

By now, too, many of his pupils were grown up, and were getting scattered abroad in the world ; and some of his classes were inevitably disbanded.

Still time went on, till at last, on meeting him casually in town, one came to fancy that, whether it was that his age was really telling upon him, or through other reasons, he was shrinking somewhat. His coat seemed surely to have unwonted and needless wrinkles. Disquieting suspicion slowly gathered that perhaps the number of his pupils might have fallen off, and living grown harder. His eyes, too, though he was cheery, and friendly as of yore, seemed to have undergone some subtle change. They looked more strained and set; and he was apt when in the street to pass one by unless addressed. Could his eyesight be failing? That would be ominous; for he had no savings to fall back upon. All had gone to the printing of his system, publishers not having proved enthusiasts. One heard, moreover, that he had been busy 'arranging' airs from popular operas for two or three instruments. What could be the cause of his reversion to such work? One could only hope it was not hunger.

To his friends, however, he would admit no difficulties, no illness. When asked—even somewhat urgently asked—how he was, he would answer, as in the old days, 'Ah, thank you, quite well.' But yet—but yet—it may have been the habit alone of self-discipline that kept him in so iron a silence as to personal troubles. It was impossible to do more than beg him, with a semblance of laughter at the remoteness of the chance, to send word if he ever did fall ill; and so at last leave matters and let him go.

Before long it was known that he had applied for a post as violin leader in a theatrical band—once more reverting to long discontinued work. But our fears were not unfounded, he had been passed over because his sight was hopelessly failing. Then within two days came the last news—this time, alas! through the newspapers. The old man had chosen not to await Fate's shears, but to sever the frayed threads himself. With final considerateness for his landlady, he had gone out from his lodgings far into the streets.

A letter was afterwards found which explained these things. He had finished resolutely the 'system' which his task-mistress Music had laid upon him. And now, though he loved gentleness and hated cruelty, he had yet not shrunk from what he regarded as a last hard duty.

Thus did the curtain fall upon the drama in which old Concordio had been so long a-fiddling; and he got up and went away.

'OUT, OUT, BRIEF CANDLE': A READING OF A PICTURE

FROM A PAINTING BY MARGARET ANDERTON

# V

# MORS JANUA VITAE: A READING OF A PICTURE

FAR into the night the priest sits there at his desk, now reading in his books of divinity, now meditating on that antique skull, brown with age and rich in lessons of mortality ; anon turning the pages of the well-thumbed old missal and softly humming some loved part of its music— till at length the guttering candle catches his eye and starts a new train of thought. How full of deep colour is that skull as the jumping flame illumines it! How rich the lights on the neighbouring copper candlestick! Nay, in the whole group, how beautiful the harmony of colours— the leaping flame, the yellow-brown skull, the deep burnished copper, and, open before him, the lovely page of the missal with its royal reds and its jet-black notes and words, and with that black rosary—three Aves and a Pater—lying over the left-hand page. Then, too, the colour of that old book on which the skull rests—green-grey, with reddish sprinkled edges ; and of the other closed

missal pushed by on the left—its crimson morocco
and its grey-green bookmarks hanging from the
yellowed edges of the leaves. These, with the
soft faded green of the table-cloth in the front,
and, behind all, the dark brown of the cabinet's
dim oak pigeon-holes, are indeed fair to the eyes.
Fair indeed to the mortal eye ; and to the inward
eye also not without significance. Does not the
neighbourhood of that unchanging, sombre skull
give the candle its rarest, most ethereal beauty ?
Is it not after looking unflinchingly into those
hollow eyes that the living flame shines purest ?
Has not some one said (in the spirit of Thomas
à Kempis) that it is by contemplating death that
life grows more lovely, more divine ; that it
is by an ever-present sense of death that life
becomes more potent, more radiant ? So (by
what strange inversion ?) it is death that leads to
the brightest beams of this present life. Is it
not death, too, that holds out to us, instead of
the flickering candle of this bodily life, the more
searching and steadfast light of the life spiritual ?
With death, then, as our light-bearer we may see
how things 'are in their nature proportioned ' ;
we may know how fleeting are life's outward
pleasures, how brief its pains. We see also how
our inward life, in measure as it is detached
from earthly encumbrances and is spent in a
daily dying to them, in meditating things not of
this world, attains a purer, a more single-eyed

vision.    Thus the life which is truest and purest is that which is ever dying.    Thus the dying to this world is the deepest, the divinest living. Wherefore, O Death, 'where is thy sting?'   It is thou that freest us from the transitory things of the body, giving us in their stead the enduring life of the spirit ; by thee alone do we enter into the life eternal.

So, far into the night, the priest sits musing.

# VI

## CONCERNING THE BOOK-PLATES OF THOMAS BEWICK

In the Bewick Collection which the late Mr. John William Pease bequeathed to the Newcastle-upon-Tyne Public Library there are many examples of Thomas Bewick's work as a designer of book-plates.

In the following pages I propose to inquire into the relation which such work bore to Bewick's other work. To this end it will be useful, if we are to see the matter in a right perspective, to recall the main events of his life, to draw attention to the things which interested him most keenly, and to record, very briefly, the main achievements upon which his great fame as a wood-engraver is generally acknowledged to rest. We shall then be in a position to turn our attention more particularly to his treatment of *ex-libris*, and may conclude by indicating the chief features of the collection that now enriches Newcastle-upon-Tyne.

The main outline of Thomas Bewick's life is, of course, widely known.

44

OAK TREE WITH DISTANT NEWCASTLE.   BY THOMAS BEWICK.

*See* 1815, *p.* 54.

Born in 1753, at Cherryburn House, near Eltringham, a hamlet on the banks of the Tyne, he was sent, when quite young, to Mickley school, so as to keep him, as he says, 'out of harm's way.' Here his first schoolmaster, who believed in the efficacy of the taws and the switch, made things somewhat too lively for him, and he frequently played truant. With his second schoolmaster, however, he got on better. On this second master's death he was taken by his father to Ovingham, to the Rev. Christopher Gregson's school. His father described him to Mr. Gregson as unguidable and unmanageable, and begged his new teacher to take charge of him, not sparing the rod. His father, by the way, though somewhat stern and harsh in his methods of training the lad, was deeply concerned for his right progress and welfare ; and in later years Bewick, in his *Memoir*, speaks of him frequently with great filial affection and appreciation.

At Ovingham Bewick seems to have got on well enough, both in the matter of beatings and in the matter of acquiring knowledge. To enliven the tedium of mastering long tasks, he used to fill his slate, the margins of his books, and any blank paper, with drawings. When paper ran short he betook himself, with a bit of chalk, to the gravestones, the floor of the church porch, and, when he got home, to the flags of the

floor and the hearthstone.　Then a friend gave
him some drawing-paper, and he started work
with pen and ink and the juice of the bramble-
berry, and still later with 'a camel-hair pencil
and shells of colours.'　His subjects were the
beasts and birds of the neighbourhood, and
hunting - scenes in which the portraits of the
hunters, the horses, and of every dog in the pack

BOOK-PLATE FOR M. ANDERSON.　BY T. BEWICK.

were faithfully delineated !　On holidays he
constantly joined hunting - parties, and thus
learnt much of the ways and appearance of birds
and beasts.　In winter months, too, he had
much tending of sheep to do and other farm-
work.　He delighted in snow-storms, and 'felt
an extreme pleasure and curiosity' in watching
for the rarer birds, which severe weather drove

from place to place in quest of shelter. He was always getting into mischievous pranks, and was full of an inexhaustible vitality. As he says: ' My life at school and at home might be considered as a life of warfare,' and punishments of various kinds were inflicted with apparently little effect. But at length Mr. Gregson, half in despair, invited the boy to dinner with him, and then by kind and frank reasoning really got hold of him, gaining more in a single friendly hour than in the months of previous severity. Bewick 'never dared to encounter another of these friendly meetings.'

His enjoyment of such things as man-fights, dog-fights, etc., gave way after a time to sympathy with the beaten victims, and even to disgust at the brutality that was often exhibited.

The ways of birds, ants, bees, fascinated him intensely, and he spent many and many an hour watching them.

Bewick's childhood, with its love of drawing and of natural history, and its indomitable vitality, has been worth adverting to, because in his case, so pre-eminently, the child was father to the man. We may now pass on more quickly.

When he was fourteen (*i.e.* in 1767) he was apprenticed to Ralph Beilby, the Newcastle engraver. He was employed for some time copying Copeland's *Ornaments*. This was the only kind of drawing upon which he ever had a lesson from any one (*Memoir*, p. 57).  He himself says : ' I was never a pupil to any drawing-master, and had not even a lesson from William Beilby, or his brother Thomas, who, along with their other profession, were also drawing-masters.' He was put to blocking-out the wood about the lines on the diagrams for the *Ladies' Diary*, and to etching sword-blades, and afterwards to a great variety of other jobs.  He learnt to fit up and temper his own tools, and adapt them to every purpose.  Beilby, though he preferred metal-work and excelled in ornamental silver engraving, undertook every kind of work, and made his pupils turn their hands to a wide range of subjects.  Bewick thought him, for this reason, the best master in the world for teaching boys, and regarded him as an ingenious, self-made artist.

They were occasionally applied to by printers to execute woodcuts.  In this branch of his business Beilby was very defective, and though he did not refuse the jobs, he did not like them. So he gave them to Bewick, to whom the opportunity thus afforded of drawing the designs on the wood was highly gratifying.  His cut of ' George and the Dragon ' for a bar-bill attracted notice, and this kind of work increased.  Orders were received for cuts to illustrate children's books ; and, before long, Bewick's time was greatly taken up with designing and cutting wood-blocks for the *Story-teller* and for books of Fables. In these fable cuts he was so successful that in 1775 he got a prize of £7, 7s. from the Society for the Encouragement of Arts—his first distinction outside Newcastle. It was left to his choice whether he would have it in a gold medal or in money. He preferred the latter ; and, as

*John Headlam, M.A.*

BOOK-PLATE. BY T. BEWICK.

he says, ' I never in my life felt greater pleasure than in presenting it to my mother. On this occasion, amongst the several congratulations of kind neighbours, those of Mr. Gregson, my old master, stood pre-eminent. He flew from Oving-ham, where the news first arrived, over to Eltring-

ham, to congratulate my father and mother ; and
the feelings and overflowings of his heart can be
better imagined than described.' This prize he
received shortly after he was out of his appren-
ticeship.

Bewick now went to live at Cherryburn, where
he had plenty of work to do, chiefly from Angus,
the Newcastle printer. He stayed at Cherryburn, employed by Angus and others, till the
summer of 1776. As he says : 'This was a time
of great enjoyment, for the charms of the country
were highly relished by me. . . . Having all my
life, at home, at school, and during my appren-
ticeship, lived under perpetual restraints, when I
then felt myself at liberty I became, as I suppose,
like a bird which had escaped from its cage.'
He spent much of his time in angling, of which
he was all his life extremely fond.

He soon started off on a walking-tour, first to
Carlisle and thence into Scotland, where the
beauty and serenity of the Highland lakes, and
the grandeur or terrific aspect of the mountains,
charmed him to ecstasy. 'It sometimes hap-
pened that by my having stopped too long on my
way in admiration of the varied prospect I met
with, that I was benighted and was obliged to
take shelter under some rocky projection, or to
lay myself down amongst the heather, till day-
light.' He made his way to Edinburgh, and
thence returned by sea to Shields.

BALL-TICKET.  BY T. BEWICK.
*Adopted as a book-plate successively by W. Garret and*
*J. W. Pease.  See 1795, 1818, pp. 54, 64.*

He stayed long enough in Newcastle to earn money to take him to London, where he arrived 1st October 1776. There he did some cuts for Isaac Taylor, Thomas Hodgson, and others, earning a good deal of money, but never managing to keep it, as he 'could not bear to see distress without relieving it.'

However, he did not like London—came to hate it, in fact—so that, as he declared to Isaac Taylor, who remonstrated with him about wanting to throw up such good prospects, he would rather enlist for a soldier, or go and herd sheep at five shillings a week all his life, than be tied to live in London. Taylor was offended at his refusal to stay, but Hodgson offered to furnish him with plenty of work in Newcastle, if he would do it. This was particularly pleasing to Bewick, who 'could not bear the thoughts of beginning business in Newcastle in opposition to [his] old master, for whom [he] had the greatest respect.' It appeared to him like the proverb, 'bring up chickens to pick out your eyes.' He returned to Newcastle by sea in June 1777.

His former master, Ralph Beilby, now offered him a partnership in his business, and this he decided to accept. He took his brother, John Bewick, as an apprentice.

Bewick thus became definitely established in Newcastle as an engraver, and his fame gradually and surely increased. The chief events of his progress may be briefly indicated in their chronological order. Certain book-plates of which the dates are known are also recorded in the list; they are printed, however, in italics.

In 1779, the first edition of Fables of the late Mr. Gay was published.

In 1784, the second edition of the Select Fables appeared. (The first edition, containing a much inferior set of cuts, had appeared in 1776.)

1789. Cut of the Chillingham Bull; also, Consett's Tour.

1790. History of Quadrupeds, 1st edition. The publication of this work was considered by Bewick to be his 'commencement of wood engraving worthy of attention.'

1791. History of Quadrupeds, 2nd edition. Ostervald's Bible (pictures engraved by Beilby and Bewick).

1792. History of Quadrupeds, 3rd edition.

1795. Poems by Goldsmith and Parnell, 1st edition (engraving done partly by Bewick).

*Ball ticket with inscription, 'Recreation is sweeter when mingled with Charity.' This cut was afterwards used as a bookplate by W. Garret, who had the inscrip-*

*tion removed and his own name and arms inserted.*

*(See the year 1818 below.)*

1796. Somervile's Chase, 1st edition (engraving done mostly by Bewick).

1797. *Book-plate for Thomas Bell (the first one dated).*

History of British Birds, vol. i. (Land Birds).

1798. Partnership with R. Beilby terminated, as from January 1.

1800. *Book-plate for Sol. Hodgson (a funeral card).*

*Book-plate for Jane Hewitson.*

1802. Somervile's Chase, 2nd edition.

*Book-plate for J. Murray, or Rev. H. Cotes (who assisted Bewick in the preparation of the letter-press for the second volume of the History of British Birds). See, however, 'Cotes,' and 'Jn. Murray' in the list of book-plates given below.*

1804. History of British Birds, vol. ii. (Water Birds).

Poems by Goldsmith and Parnell, *another edition.*

1805. History of British Birds, 2nd edition.

*Book-plate for R. Murray.* Warren gives this year as the approximate date.

1806. The Hermit of Warkworth, 1st edition. Engraving done by Bewick.

1807. History of Quadrupeds, 5th edition.
   Hermit of Warkworth, 2nd edition.
1809. History of British Birds, 3rd edition.
1810. *Book-plate of Carlisle family.* (Warren's date.)
   *Book-plate of James Charlton.*
   *Book-plate of Robert Southey, the Poet.*
1811. History of Quadrupeds, 6th edition.
1815. *Oak-tree with distant Newcastle, adopted in* 1904 *as the book-plate of the Newcastle-upon-Tyne Reference Library. It was engraved for Mr. Falla, and passed successively into the hands of Rev. J. F. Bigge, Robert Robinson, J. W. Pease, and the Newcastle Public Library. The words ' Arbor Scientiæ, Ex Libris Public Reference Library, Newcastle-upon-Tyne (established* 1884*), and the initials ' T. B.,' have, on the book-plate, been printed below. A year or two before this I find that a stereo of the same cut had been adopted by Mr. J. G. Angus as his book-plate.*
1816. History of British Birds, 4th edition.
1818. Fables of Æsop and others, 1st edition.
   Two of the 'Newcastle Reprints,' *viz.* Chorographia ; or a Survey of Newcastle-upon-Tyne ; and, An Account of the Great Floods in 1771 and 1815.
   The illustration on the title-pages of these

two tracts afterwards formed the book-plate of W. Garret. It had originally (according to Robinson's *Thomas Bewick*, p. 306) been a ticket of admission to a ball, and was executed in 1795. When afterwards the block was in the possession J. W. Pease, it became in turn one of his book-plates. He evidently had Garret's inscription and arms filled up, and he substituted his own by means apparently of a second printing. That the block was not thereby damaged is evident from the impression taken directly from the block quite recently, and here reproduced. (See p. 64.)

1820. History of Quadrupeds, 7th edition.
Two of the 'Newcastle Reprints,' *viz.* The Siege of Newcastle, by W. Lithgow; and, His Majesties passing through the Scots armie.
The cut on the title-pages of the two last-named pamphlets was used as a book-plate by J. T. Brockett.

1821. History of British Birds, 5th edition.
Supplement to above.
*Book-plate of B. Liddell.*

1824. *Memorial cut for William Robson.*
History of Quadrupeds, 8th edition.

1826. History of British Birds, 6th edition.

1827. Vignettes, by Thomas Bewick. This con-

tains nearly all the vignettes of the Quadrupeds and Birds, without letterpress.
Newcastle Reprint: The Scots Martch from Barwick to Newcastle.

Bewick died in 1828, at the age of seventy-five. His mother had died in February 1785, his father in November 1785; his brother John, too, had died in December 1795.

He married a Miss Isabella Elliot of Ovingham, in April 1786. He had four children—a son, Robert Elliot Bewick, who achieved some fame as an engraver, and three daughters, Elizabeth, Jane, and Isabella. His wife died in 1826.

If we turn now more exclusively to the bookplates which Bewick cut, it will be tolerably clear that he regarded them merely as incidental work. His main concern was with birds, and beasts, and landscape vignettes. These latter he was able to adapt most happily to the needs (shall we say in his own phrase?) of 'the book-mad gentry.' He does not, to our recollection, even mention the book-plates in his *Memoir*. And yet, how attractive they are! As Warren, speaking of the brothers Bewick, well says: 'Very charming are their *ex-libris* vignettes. They show us ruins, rocks, deep foliage, or time-corroded boles, flowing river, distant spire and mountain. They give actual Tyneside scenes, views of Newcastle,

St. Nicholas's Tower, Jarrow Church. Unluckily, the armorial shield is far too often present, intruding itself into fishing-scenes and similar incongruous situations. But for this, the orderer of the book-plate rather than the engraver was to blame.'

As already mentioned, the earliest dated book-plate by Thomas Bewick was that of T. Bell, 1797—a date, as Warren says, 'which shows that the Bewicks followed rather than originated a taste and style already popular, which they afterwards brought to such perfection.' Again, he says on p. 182: 'In Thomas Bewick the new landscape school [of book-plate designers] found its most varied and original interpreter. . . . No one could make more than Bewick of a small and circumscribed space. . . . [His] special genius *in minimis* gained him a multitude of book-plate commissions; a large percentage of which, however, were local orders. Some critics, however, like Walpole, and some poets, like Southey, had the good taste to employ him from a distance. Accordingly, between seventy and eighty *ex-libris*, executed by Thomas Bewick, are known to exist.'

Warren's book was published in 1880, and his estimate of the number is probably correct. Hugo in his *Bewick Collector*, published in 1866-8 (pp. 305-22, and, in the Supplement, pp. 152-5), mentions eighty-five book plates; but five of these are by Robert and John. Again, it is true that the Sale Catalogue of Hugo's collection, issued in 1877, speaks (p. 41) of his ' collection of upwards of Two Hundred rare Armorial and Vignette Private Book-Plates, executed for private gentlemen, displaying some of the happiest effects of Bewick's genius, and exceedingly scarce, many almost unattainable.' The list, however (which after all is only a sale list), certainly includes one plate by Robert Bewick and one by John Bewick, and also includes, in its total of ' upwards of two hundred,' many duplicates. This collection of book-plates passed into the hands of Mr. J. W. Pease, and is now in the Newcastle Public Library as part of the Pease Bequest. The plates are printed on various materials—on yellow and white China paper, on satin, on vellum, etc.

The following is a list of them,[1] arranged alphabetically according to the owners' names. The descriptions are in some instances taken from Hugo, though as a rule fuller details are given than he furnished.

Where the name is included within quotation marks, the inscription is found in the plate, Naturally, however, surnames do not, in the plate, precede Christian names.

Adamson (John).    Ruins of Gothic arch and

---

[1] I am much indebted to Mr. W. H. Gibson, Assistant Librarian in Newcastle, for the help he gave me when I was preparing this list.

trees. St. Nicholas's Church tower in distance.

Affleck (J. H.). Plain shield (with name, ' J. H. Affleck, Newcastle-upon-Tyne '), flowers and foliage. *Copper-plate.*

'Anderson (John), St. Petersburg.' In the foreground, a sportsman on horseback, by the water's edge; in the background, a field and houses. Name on rock to left.

(This was afterwards used as a vignette in the Land Birds; see p. 149 of 1826 edition.)

'Anderson (John), jun.' Fishing scene: man among trees on top of rock. Name on rock.

'Anderson (Mattw.), St. Petersburg.' Tree on a rock (which is inscribed with the name), Tyne and distant Newcastle. The block for this is in the Collection. (See illustration, p. 46.)

'Archbold (J.).' Trees, rock, and river; mill in the distance. Name on rock. *Copper-plate.* See Atkinson (H.), below. See also Binns (T.), below.

Armstrong (William). Rock with trees and distant view of Newcastle; shield with coat of arms supported against the rock. This cut was subsequently altered and used as a vignette on the title-page of Bewick's *Memoir,* 1862.

'Atkinson (Buddle).' Fishing scene: trees and

stream ; shield with coat-of-arms beneath
trees. *Copper-plate.* Assigned by Hugo
to T. Bewick, but by Mr. J. Vinycomb, with
somewhat greater probability, to G. F.
Robinson, chief engraver to the Lamberts.

'Atkinson (George).' Arms alone. *Copper-plate.*
Attributed by Hugo to T. Bewick, but by
Mr. J. Vinycomb to Lambert.

'Atkinson (H.).' Trees, rock, and river; mill in
the distance. *Copper-plate.* Almost iden-
tical with that of Archbold, above. See also
Binns (T.), below.

'Bell (John), Gateshead.' Angel (rather cor-
pulent) resting on clouds, blowing a trumpet.
The ink of the name seems somewhat different from that of the design. A poor
engraving.

Bell (Matthew), M.P. Shield of arms. Used
for the dedication to Hubberthorn's *Travels*,
from a copy of which it is cut out.

'Bell (Thomas), 1797.' An oval with the name,
leaning against an oak; Newcastle in distance.

Bigge (——). Figure of Liberty sitting beneath
a tree. Motto: 'Truth, Liberty, Virtue.'
This cut appeared on the title-page of each
number of *The Oeconomist*, 1798-9.

'Bilton (Willm.), Newcastle.' Trees, with a
shield of arms. *Copper-plate.* Assigned to
T. Bewick by Hugo.

'Binns (T.), Leeds.' Almost like Archbold's book-plate, reversed. See also M. Hewitson's book-plate, below; and H. Atkinson's, above.

Brockett (J. T.). Norman doorway, with shield of arms. Motto: 'Invictus maneo.' See Fenwick, below.

—— Arms alone. Motto: 'Invictus maneo.'

—— Arms alone, with name John Trotter Brockett underneath. *Copper-plate*. Not mentioned by Hugo.

Carlisle, *Mr.* [so described by Hugo, who obtained this impression from Miss Bewick]. An old oak stump with Newcastle in the distance. Baron's coronet and motto: 'Fuimus.' Approximate date, 1810 (Warren, p. 184).

Carr (Thomas). Trees and a rock, inscribed 'Thos. Carr, Newcastle. No.    .' *Copperplate*.

Chapman (——). Arms alone.

'Charlton (Chas.), M.D.' View of Tynemouth from the sea. Motto: 'Succurrere disco.' *Copper-plate*.

Charlton (James). Trees, and a rock inscribed 'James Charlton, Gateshead. No.    .' Newcastle in distance. Signed 'T. Bewick sculpt.' Approximate date, 1810 (Warren, p. 184). *Copper-plate*.

'Clapham (A.).' Trees, and a rock with name.

Tyneside scene, with cathedral in distance. *Copper-plate.*

'Cook (Joseph).' Branch of a tree, with shield of arms. Spire of St. Nicholas on left.

? 'Cotes (Rev. H.), Vicar, Bedlington, 1802.' The authority for this book-plate is simply the word of Mr. W. Garret,[1] whose descriptions of Bewickiana were at times open to criticism.[2] Fishing scene ; rock with trees in foreground. Name on one face of the rock, and on another the inscription : 'Flumina amem sylvasque inglorius.' This was subsequently used, without any name, as a tailpiece to the Water Birds, p. 370 (1804). Bewick had a great liking for the cut. Garret, as quoted by Hugo, says that in the original form impressions are very rare. The two copies in this Collection are, it is probable, not genuine ; and one may even doubt the existence of any book-plate cut for Cotes. The words ' Rev. H. Cotes, Vicar, Bedlington, 1802,' are very roughly cut, and might have been inserted subsequently. See Murray (Jn.), below.

Coulthard (John). River scene ; tree, and to the left a rock (inscribed ' John Coulthard. No. .'). *Copper-plate.*

---

[1] See Hugo, No. 1991.

[2] See, for example, entry No. 102 in the *Catalogue of the Bewick Collection* (Pease Bequest), published in Newcastle in 1904.

BOOK-PLATE FOR JOHN FENWICK.   BY T. BEWICK.
*See p. 63.*

Croker (R. E.). Arms alone, and motto : 'Deus alit eos.' Name printed below. Signed 'Bewick sculpt.' For this cut Bewick received £5, and Hugo (p. 533) speaks of a letter, written by Miss Bewick, but signed by Thomas Bewick, acknowledging receipt (June 26, 1822), and expressing his gratification that the work had met with Croker's approbation.

Culley (——). Hunt-card for meeting of Mr. Culley's beagles. Beagle running past trees and rock. Signed 'T. Bewick & Son.' *Copper-plate.*

'Davidson (John), Newcastle, Cl. P., Northumberland.' Arms alone. Motto : 'Sapienter si sincere.' *Copper-plate.*

'Doeg (Alexr.).' Ship on the stocks.

'Donkin (Armorer).' Rock and trees, with a spring of water. Shield with arms supported against the rock. Motto : 'In labore quies.'

'Ewart (Francis).' Shield of arms. Motto : 'Pro deo rege et patria.' *Copper-plate.*

Fenwick (John). Norman doorway with shield of arms. On the scroll, 'A Fenwyke, A Fenwyke. Tous jours loyal.' Somewhat similar in general design to Brockett's bookplate.

'Fryer (W.).' Rock, river, and trees, with St. Nicholas's Church in the distance. Name on face of rock. *Copper-plate.*

Garret (W.).   Rock and trees; shield of arms in
foreground ;   Newcastle   in   distance   across
the Tyne.   Motto :  ' Rather break than bend.'
This cut was not done for Garret, but was at
first,   as   explained   above   (under   the   years
1795 and 1818), a ball ticket, and was subsequently used for other purposes.   The block
itself   is   in   the   Collection,   and   was   adopted
by Mr. J. W. Pease as one of his book-plates.
Green (J.).   An oval inscribed ' J. Green.   No.
' ; with a little drapery—very rough.
' Hawks (Geoᵉ.).'   A hawk standing on a rock in
the   foreground ;   in   the   background   a   hill
with castle and trees.   This copy was pre-
sented to the Newcastle Public Library in
April 1905, by Mrs. Geo. Hawks, Junr., who
says in the letter accompanying the impression :  ' It   was   given   by   Bewick   himself   to
my  father-in-law,  George  Hawks  of  Red-
heugh.'   Not mentioned by Hugo.
' Headlam (John).'   Shield with arms, supported
against a rock at the foot of a tree ; castle in
background. Motto: ' Intellectu et innocentia.'
*Copper-plate.*   The plate itself is in the Newcastle Collection.   Not mentioned by Hugo.
Hewitson (Hy.).   An oval, inscribed ' H. H.,'
among foliage.
' Hewitson (Jane).'   Rock, tree, and river scene.
Branch   inscribed   ' Jane   Hewitson ' ;   rock
inscribed ' April 24, 1800.'

BOOK-PLATE FOR THOMAS HODGSON.　BY T. BEWICK.

'Hewitson (M.).' A close copy of T. Binns's book-plate.

Hodgson (Solomon). Churchyard with yew-tree overshadowing a tomb inscribed 'Sol. Hodgson, obt. 4 April 1800, Æ. 39.' Memorial book-plate. Signed 'T. Bewick, sc.'

Hodgson (Thomas). Tyneside scene, showing St. Nicholas's Church and Windmill Hills, from the west, within a border of trees.

—— Tyneside scene, with Newcastle in the distance, and with shield of arms in foreground leaning against a tree. Motto : 'Sine veritate nunquam.'

'Johnson, Byker.' Arms alone, and inscription : 'Experto crede.' *Copper-plate.*

'Kerrich (Jno.), Harleston.' Trees and a rock inscribed with name. Tynemouth in distance.

Liddell (B.). Tyneside scene with trees in foreground and a rock inscribed '16 February 1821.' Newcastle in distance. There are two states, the rock in one being considerably enlarged, and the name 'B. Liddell' added below. One impression of each.

'Liddell (Rev. H. G.).' Arms alone. Motto: 'Fama semper vivit.' *Copper-plate.* The plate itself is in the Newcastle Collection. Not mentioned in Hugo.

? Losh (Geo.), Saltwellside. Trees, rock, and spring. Impression without name. Pro-

E

bably No. 2056 in Hugo, since it was in its alphabetical position in the album described in the Hugo Sale Catalogue.

'Losh (James).' Rock with name, and trees, with Newcastle in the distance. *Copper-plate.*

'Marley (John).' Arms alone. *Copper-plate.*

'Moises (Edwd.), A.M.' Shield of arms with books, etc. Scroll: 'Fallentis semita vitæ.' *Copper-plate.*

'Murray (John).' Shield of arms amidst foliage. Scroll: 'Furth Fortune and fill the Fetters.'

'Murray (Jn.), Surgeon, Newcastle, 1802.' This is the same cut as described under Cotes's name. The inscription on the rock appears to have been printed direct from the block. The plate is not mentioned by Warren nor by Hugo, but bears every appearance of genuineness.

One may hazard the suggestion that the Cotes book-plate, as described above, was manufactured by a dealer from impressions of this cut, for there are traces of the removal (possibly by chemicals) of the words 'Jn. Murray, Surgeon, Newcastle,' and the substitution in a different ink of the words 'Rev. H. Cotes, Vicar, Bedlington.' The date 1802, however, has been left. Signed 'T. B.'

Murray (R.). Oak, shield and armour; druidical remains in the distance. Motto: ' Non in visco fides sed in deo.' Warren gives 1805 as the approximate date.

' Philipson (Nicholas John).' Arms alone. Scroll : ' Fide non Fraude.' *Copper-plate*.

' Reay (Henry Utrick), Esq., Killingworth.' Shield of arms on an ivied wall.

' Robson (William).' Arms alone. Motto: ' Be just and fear not.' *Copper-plate*.

—— Memorial cut. An oval in oblong border with the following inscription: 'Wm. Robson, a Newcastle worthy, a refuge for the distressed, a patron of ingenuous youth, a promoter of general education, a devoted friend to civil and religious liberty. He died Feb. 16, 1824, aged 80.'

' Row (Wm.).' Arms alone. Motto: ' Fortitudo et prudentia.' *Copper-plate*.

Sanders (J. W.). Shield of arms supported against the base of some ruins. Motto: ' Esse quam videri.'

' Sherwood (T.).' Trees, and a rock inscribed with the name. Hugo does not mention this ; yet it looks like Bewick's work. It is mentioned in the Sale Catalogue.

' Sill (James), Liverpool.' Trees, and inscribed rock.

' Simpson (R.).' Trees, inscribed rock, two birds wading in stream.

Southey (Robert). Trees, rock (supporting shield, and spring. Motto : ' In labore quies.' Below are the words, ' R. Southey, Bristol, 1802.' Warren gives the date of Southey's book-plate as 1810. Hugo does not mention the date. In this impression the ink of the signature looks slightly fainter than that of the block itself. In all probability the signature was not a part of the block at all, but was inserted by Kerslake, a bookseller, on the front page of whose catalogue, dated 1845, the plate is printed. The signature does not appear in the reproduction given in Hardy's *Book-Plates*, p. 81.

'Stamford (H.).' Trees and bushes surrounding a statue of a stag on a pedestal.

'Stawpert (James), Willington.' Oval border of leaves, etc., enclosing name. Below is written by hand, ' Literæ secundas res ornant, adversis perfugium et solatium præbent.'

'Stobart (John).' A tripod, with the legs inscribed 'Veritas, Libertas, Virtus,' supporting a globe inscribed ' Bonum Publicum.' At the foot of the tripod are a plough, sword, book, cap of liberty, etc. In the distance are cottages, a three-barred gate, trees, etc. See Taylor (Wm.).

Straker (John ?). View of Jarrow Church and adjoining ruins ; shield of arms in foreground.

Straker (John). Chapel in Newcastle Castle; shield with the same arms as in preceding, except that here the shield is surmounted by a galloping horse. This cut is on the title-page of *Memoirs of the Public Life of Sir Walter Blackett, Bart.,* . . . 1819, of which John Straker was the author.

'Swarley (Richd.), Newcastle.' Motto: 'Libertas auro pretiosior.' Two female figures with cornucopia, shield, cap of liberty, etc. *Copper-plate.*

Taylor (Wm.). Similar to Stobart's book-plate, with the foreground differently arranged and a background of trees only. Signed 'T. Bewick sculp.' From Hugo's quotation of John Bell (under No. 2101) it would seem that this was the original design, and that 'a copy was made somewhat different for Mr. John Stobart, attorney, Gateshead.' The name Wm. Taylor is suffixed to one of the two impressions.

'Thomas (William).' River scene, rock inscribed with name, and plough and harrow in foreground.

Thompson (Samuel). Trees, spring, and rock inscribed 'Saml. Thompson, Newcastle. No. .' *Copper-plate.*

'Thompson (T.).' Trees and a rock inscribed with name: a river scene, with Newcastle (probably) in the distance.

Walpole (Honble. Horace). View of Strawberry Hill in framework of foliage, which supports a shield of arms and motto: 'Fari quæ sentiat.' This differs in the arrangement of the foliage forming the border, in the position of the shield, and in some smaller details from the representation given in Castle's *English Book-Plates*, p. 146. Castle's remarks about the plate which he reproduces are interesting, and, as they might apply to any copy of the Strawberry Hill vignette, they may be quoted. He says: 'This plate has been attributed to Bewick, but, as Mr. Austin Dobson has pointed out to me, if any of the Strawberry Hill plates were executed by the Northumbrian engraver, they are simply exact copies of the vignette copper which appears on the title-page of Gray's *Odes* (the first book issued from the Strawberry Hill Press) in 1757. In that year Bewick was only four years old. Horace Walpole died in 1797, at a time when Bewick was most busy about this sort of work, but it is not likely that this original draughtsman should have copied an old device.'

Exception may be taken to part of this. To begin with, as already mentioned, the plates are not exact copies. Then, too, a reference to the present list under the names

Archbold, Atkinson, Binns and Hewitson, Brockett and Fenwick, Stobart and Taylor ; a recollection moreover of the close general similarity of many of the book-plates (tree, rock, river scene, with Newcastle in the distance) will amply show that Bewick was not averse from copying, with very slight alterations, at least his own work. His treatment, too, of the illustrations to the *Oxford Sausage* (1814 and 1815 editions), and of the cuts in Croxall's *Fables* when issuing his *Æsop's Fables* (1818), will show that he had no objection to copying, on occasion, other people's work.

'Watson (H.).' Urn, upon a monument inscribed with name, amongst trees. *Copper-plate.*

? 'Wilson (Rt.).' Trees upon rock inscribed with name ; urn, and river scene. Hugo ascribes this to Thomas Bewick, but upon the urn are the initials I. B., probably for John Bewick.

'Wright (Wm.).' An oval slightly ornamented containing the following :—

'WM. WRIGHT'S BOOK

' In Greenland's freezing climate I have been,
West India's sultry plains likewise I 've seen ;
But now, in riper years, not giv'n to roam,
I rest content to read my books at home.'

Young (Thomas). Exterior view of a transept

of a church ; shield of arms in foreground.
This is printed upon the title-page of Young's
*British Literature*, 1827.

Miss Boyd, in her *Bewick Gleanings* (p. 66 *sq.*),
speaks very highly of Thomas Bewick's book-
plates, ' on which he delighted to bestow infinite
pains, and to enrich with his most delicate delinea-
tion of foliage.' With these blocks, she says, ' he
used occasionally to oblige his particular friends.'
She quotes, too, Mr. Pearson : ' The book
vignettes and armorial bearings are worthy of
close observation. Many of these were done for
Bewick's private and cherished friends. To him
such souvenirs were not the subjects of mere
professional toil ; they were labours of love ; he
lavished his highest gifts on them. His exuberant
fancy revelled in ingenious delineations, and his
intimate acquaintance with natural scenery imbued his designs with a sort of artistic fascination.'

Well, this is a little like ' fine writing,' and
Pearson's discrimination was perhaps not always
unimpeachable.[1] We have already seen that
there was a good deal of repetition among Bewick's
book-plates, and there is also a fair amount of
poor work. We have seen, moreover, that Mr.
Croker paid him £5 for his cut, and Miss Boyd
(p. 68) states (though without mentioning the

---

[1] See, for instance, the *Academy* of March 22, 1884.

source of her information) that ' Bewick was in the habit of charging more for these book-blocks than his ordinary prices.'

Still, there are undoubtedly many lovely pieces of work amongst the book-plates, and those ' book-mad gentry' whom Bewick *obliged*, had on the whole abundant reason to be gratified by what he did for them.

There is not, perhaps, much evidence to show that Bewick regarded this sort of work, for the most part, otherwise than he regarded ordinary work for ordinary customers. As Hugo says : ' It was only natural that advantage should be taken of his exquisite powers by the professional and commercial men of his great town and neighbourhood—by the former for book-plates, memorial cuts, and similar objects ; by the latter for notices of exhibitions, bill-heads, shop-cards, bar-bills, coal certificates, etc. ; and by both for various societies and companies, the members of which they jointly composed' (p. 303).

Bewick's total output of work during his long life was extraordinarily large. Apart from the great number of wood-blocks which he cut for the *Birds*, *Quadrupeds*, *Æsop's Fables*, and *Select Fables*, etc., there are the miscellaneous books on which he worked (including Somervile's *Chase*, Goldsmith and Parnell's *Poems*, etc. etc.). There are also his water-colour paintings, his coal certificates and so forth—to say nothing of all the arrangements connected with printing and publishing his books and the management of the details of his business.

As a mere matter of quantity, then, the seventy or eighty or ninety little book-plates with which he is credited do not bulk largely in proportion to the whole; and, to put the matter succinctly, it would seem that although in the course of his work Bewick did a few beautiful copper-plate *ex-libris*, and although he cut for book-lovers a fair number of wood-block vignettes which bear the distinctive marks of his delightful genius, yet he regarded them as something by the way; they were like pleasant backwaters from the main current of his life's achievements. His fame chiefly rests on the vignettes proper (viz., not those adapted to the purposes of book collectors), and on the Birds.

BOOK-PLATE BY T. BEWICK

THE ISLE OF ULYSSES

FROM A DRAWING BY LILLIE CLAY

# VII

## IN THE ISLE OF ULYSSES:
## A FANTASY

FAR away in the blue Ionian Sea there is an island called the Isle of Ulysses. Hither at last, after the fret and fume of city life, one may voyage. Here one may sleep long, dreamless sleeps; here scramble idly among the cypresses, and breathe deep draughts of the mellow southern air. Here one may bathe in a sea that is warm and tranquil, and sit peacefully beside the blue tideless water, whilst the fever of chafing thoughts dies down, and the restless eagerness to get things accomplished gives place to an unhurrying patience.

There are but three or four houses on the little island. In one of them you will live under the care of a bright, ingenious, and passably honest Greek. Anon he will tempt you to explore the neighbouring Corfu (which you still think of as Corcyra) in some old-world little craft. He will teach you to handle the sails, to scud before the wind, to hug the shores when there is any sign of sudden storms. You will have Homeric

adventures in miniature, and the *Odyssey* will
take on a new and actual charm.   In turn you,
even you, will be driven from your course by
baffling winds, and will spend whole nights in
the friendly covert of the woods, your boat
beached safe from the waves below you.   As the
spirit of adventure re-awakens within you, you
will be less satisfied with the brief range of
Dmitri's enterprises, and will want to go further
and further into the heart of the sea or of the
neighbouring lands.   You will begin to throw
the net of your plans wider, and instead of only
running before favourable winds or in the trend
of circumstances, as Dmitri would have you do,
you will begin once more to rule your circumstances, to turn them to account, and to make
one aspect of them or another subserve your own
deliberate ends.

Then, after long days afloat or ashore, you will
turn with renewed delight to the books you have
brought with you.   Their attraction will become
more potent, their romance will satisfy you again
and again more fully, till at last you will begin
even to tire a little of your explorations and of
the busy external life which for the most part
you are leading.   Memories, too, concerning the
happier episodes of your work in that far-off
home of yours will gradually obtrude themselves ;
and now they will be not unwelcome guests.   The
little daily inconveniences you have here to put

up with, which at first, if thought of at all, were merely amusing, are becoming more noticeable, and even a little irksome. Perhaps after all there were advantages in the distant town life you were so rejoiced to leave. At least you had not this annoyance to endure, or that bit of Greek lying to correct. The ways of thought of your own folk are in the long run more akin to your nature; and the first sunny picturesqueness of your Greeks has begun to pall. It would be pleasant enough, pretty soon, to return for a while and see how things are going on. So you resolve to have a week or two more of long days in the sunshine, and of bathing, and a few more boating or fishing expeditions with your noisy, ready-witted crews; and then, hey! for the deep, cool plunge once more amidst innumerable books. As for the troubles and vexations you endured in your work—well, on reconsideration they do not seem to have been so very intolerable. After all, they are the common lot of man; and your worries, compared to those of some people you know, were perhaps rather insignificant. The grim mountains of Difficulty are already, in your more distant and larger view, shrinking into molehills. You smile at all the nervous bitterness they caused you. The time is almost come when, glad at heart once more, refreshed in mind and alert in body, you can return to your natural and more permanent occupations.

# VIII

## TWO MINOR BOOKS OF EMBLEMS

On one small shelf at home I keep half a
dozen of my books that seem to appeal mutely
for a leisured investigation. They are for
the most part what may be termed 'forgotten
volumes'—volumes that one seldom heeds in a
second-hand catalogue, but which, whilst quietly
conning the less obvious shelves of a friendly
bookseller, one may chance to light upon and
find noteworthy. But somehow the kind of alert
leisure which they claim, and which one per-
petually hopes to find, say in the summer during
a holiday, or at latest in the winter—when one
shall be free from the distractions of daily work,
and able to capture each book's significance, and
record it to pleasure a friend or so—this leisure
seems, like many another hope, elusive as the
*ignis fatuus*. Wherefore, lest the time be spent
in vain postponement, it were better to make an
occasion forcibly rather than to expect it pas-
sively. To our task, then.

Two of the little volumes will suffice; and we

will consider this one first—a book of emblems, in old brown calf. It is five inches high, and about three and a quarter wide. Here is its title —Latin first, then French :—' Amoris | Divini et humani | Antipathia | E Variis sacrae scripturae locis deprōpta | Emblematis suis expressa | Et SS. PP. authoritatibus | illustrata. | Les Effects Divers | de l'Amour diuin et humain | richement exprimez par petits | Emblemes tires des SS. Escritures | et des SS. Peres. | Le tout mis en latin et françois. | A Paris, | Chez Guillaume le Noir, rue St. Iacques, | à la Rose blanche couronnee.   1628.'

The whole page is engraved, and the title is enclosed in a border of delicately wrought emblems, many of which recur later in the book. There is, *e.g.*, a heart transfixed by two arrows, and smoking (as with the incense of love); there are bows and arrows, flags, drums, swords, guns, a cross, a lamb, and so forth.   And at the foot of the border are the words, ' Mich. van Lochom fecit et excud.'

Lochom, in fact, is the author of the book, the scope of which he expounds more at length in a quaintly attractive dedication to Messire Charles Perrochel, Seigneur de Grandchamp, Secrétaire de sa Majesté, etc. etc.   The little volume has, he says, a desire ' to satisfy the innocent curiosity of devout and religious souls, and especially of those who keep the thorny path of virtue ; who, borne on the wings of a blameless ambition to perfect themselves, seek nothing more passionately than the forming themselves on some model of piety, so that they may thence take a generous flight and be carried to the summit of all covetable things, even the love of God. And I think that these little emblems, chosen for the most part from the Holy Scriptures so as to express the various effects of Divine Love and Human Love, will furnish all kinds of men with a motive so strong that they shall desire the charms of the one and mistrust the deceitful attractions of the other. And I feel sure that every one will gather from them feelings blent of sweetness and contentment. . . . One may see here, moreover, as on an ample stage alive with discourse and enriched with various characters, the stratagems and warlike surprises not of a Scipio or a Hannibal, a Cæsar or a Pompey, but of the two highest Kings that were ever seen ; and the spectacle is no less majestic than the most exalted things of the world, seeing that there is at stake not the conquest of a handful of earth but that of an entire kingdom, whose possession is as everlasting as eternity itself. . . . All that I have said, Sir, makes me hope that you will find diversion that is pious and worthy in itself, and that affords some ease to your mind when busied in serious affairs, as often as you turn lightly over the contents of this little volume . . .'

[' Le desir qu'il à de contenter la curiosité
innocente des ames deuotes et religieuses ; &
nommément de celles qui tiennēt le chemin
épineux de la vertu, & qui portées sur les aisles
d'une ambition irreprochable de se rendre par-
faictes, ne cherchent rien plus passionnément
qu'à se former sur quelque modele de piete, pour
de là prendre un essort genereux, & se porter au
comble de toutes les choses desirables, qui est
l'amour de Dieu.  Et i'estime que ces petits
emblemes, tirez pour la pluspart des sainctes
Escritures, pour exprimer les effects diuers de
l'Amour diuin et humain, fourniront un motif
assez puissant à toute sorte de personnes pour
desirer les attraits aimables de l'un, & se deffier
des appas trompeurs de l'autre : Et m'asseure
qu'un chacun en ressentira des effects accom-
pagnez de douceur et de contentement. . . . Aussi
pourra-t'on veoir icy comme sur un ample theatre
autant animé de discours, qu'enrichy de diuers
personnages, les stratagemes & surprises guer-
rieres non d'un Scipion ny d'un Annibal, non
d'un Cesar ny d'un Pompée, mais des deux plus
puissans Roys qui se virent iamais, dont le spectacle n'est moins remply de Majesté que les
choses plus releuées du monde, puis qu'il n'y va
pas de la conqueste d'une poignée de terre, ains
d'un Royaume tout entier, la possession duquel
est aussi perdurable que l'eternité mesme. . . .
Tout ce que i'ay dit, Monsieur, . . . me donne

F

esperance que ce vous sera un diuertissement aussi pieux qu'il est honneste, donnant quelque relasche à vostre esprit occupé dans les affaires serieuses, de parcourir legerement le contenu en ce petit volume. . . .']

Let us examine a little more closely how Lochom's booklet is designed to satisfy the aims here set forth—contenting the innocent curiosity of devout and religious minds; expressing the different effects of divine and human love; providing an experience in which sweetness and contentment mingle; and giving diversion that is alike pleasing and pious.

To begin with, the book consists of about fifty emblems. Each emblem has a leaf to itself, and has, as a rule, a short Latin quotation with a poetical French version underneath. Facing the plate (on the left) are further Latin quotations (one, two, sometimes three), while on the leaf following the plate are French paraphrases in verse. My copy is unfortunately not quite complete : some plates before No. 48 are missing, possibly the three afterwards are insertions. They have been carefully pasted down on blank pages before rebinding ; but the preceding Latin quotations and the subsequent French versions are missing ; and the designs, though still Lochom's, are in a heavier style, and certainly afford less 'douceur et contentement' than the earlier designs.

In the first forty-eight emblems then (or in those that remain of them in my copy), the true value of the book is seen. The drawing and the shading are wonderfully minute and delicate ; and if the perspective is at times a little extraordinary, the resulting quaintness seems almost to enhance the general charm. The symbolism, too, which is often as strangely crude as the metaphors of mediæval Church poetry, has a certain half-repellent attraction. It is so curious, yet so *raw*. One perceives how the possibilities of violent bodily suffering have been ransacked to express the religious emotions.

Emblem 24 is called Love's Biscuit (*biscoctum amoris*). The picture shows a furnace in which the fire is flaming fiercely, while the smoke escapes in a thick cloud from a hole which serves as a chimney in the brickwork at the back. There are two little figures, Christ being one, the other (in a woman's form) representing a human soul whom he loves. Christ is shown holding by a long handle a shovel, on which the woman places her heart, that it may be pushed into the flames and get cooked. The Latin which is being illustrated runs thus : ' Probasti cor meum, et igne me examinasti.' (Thou hast proved my heart, and hast tried me with fire.) The French paraphrase of it all is as follows :—

' Qu'il est ioly ce diuin boulanger :
Mais croyez-vous qu'il oseroit manger

Ce cœur, qu'il pense cuire dedans son four ?
Cela s'entend, car il a tousiours fain,
Et ne se paist iamais que de ce pain,
Qu'il cuit luy-mesme au feu de son Amour.'

(How charming is that divine baker !   But
would he, think you, dare to eat that heart which
he is minded to cook in his furnace?   Certainly
he would ; for he is ever hungry, and feeds only
on this bread which he cooks himself at the fire
of his love.)

In emblem 25, 'The Polishing of Love,' the
figures are as before.   The quotation is from
Hugo, In Prov. 25 : ' E corde meo aufer rubi-
ginem, Domine, nempe vanitatis, falsitatis, et
superfluitatis.' (Remove the rust from my heart,
O Lord, even the rust of vanity, deceit, and super-
fluity.)   Christ is shown half sitting on the
woodwork of a little travelling grindstone, turning the wheel with his foot, and grinding or
polishing against the revolving stone a human
heart, handed to him by the woman, who, mildly
curious, is pouring from a small jug liberal water
on the wheel.   Christ's face is that of a little boy
demurely enjoying himself.

Emblem 26 is called ' The Bath of Love.'   The
quotations illustrated are : ' Lava à malitia cor
tuum, ut salua fias.' ('Wash thine heart from
wickedness, that thou mayest be saved,' Jer. iv.
14), and ' Dealba me Domine, et munda cor
meum, ut dealbatus in sanguine Agni gaudiis

perfruar sempiternis.' (Make me white, O Lord,
and cleanse my heart, that being whitened in the
blood of the Lamb I may enjoy everlasting gladness.) To explain this, Christ is represented
standing on the stump of a low hexagonal pillar
which rises out of a hexagonal bath. From
hands, side, and feet spout streams of blood, so
that the bath is full. At the side stands the little
figure of the woman dipping a heart in the blood,
and rubbing it with a napkin. Below is this
French paraphrase :—

> ' Je laue mon cœur dans ce bain
> Pour le loger dans vostre sein.'

(I wash my heart in this bath in order to lodge it
within your bosom.)

In these emblems, unless 'sweet laughter'
intervene, or unless religious emotion dull the
critical faculty, Lochom's symbolism is realistic
to the verge of grisliness. It reminds one, as I
say, in its violent metaphors, of some of the early
Church poetry. Compare it, for instance, with
such lines as these of St. Bernard :—

> ' Qui te gustant, esuriunt ;
> qui bibunt, adhuc sitiunt.'

(Those who taste thee are still an-hungered, and
those who drink are still athirst) ; or with the
lines in the 'Stabat Mater' :—

> ' Fac me plagis vulnerari,
> Cruce hac inebriari.'

(Make me . . . to be drunk with this cross); or, again, with these lines (once more of St. Bernard) :—

> ' Quem tuus amor ebriat
> Novit quid Jesus sapiat.'

(He whom thy love makes drunk, knows what Jesus tastes like.)

In certain other pictures, however, Lochom's realism has, through defects of perspective and the like, more obviously comic qualities. Take No. 2, for example, in which two archers, each furnished with wings, are trying their skill. The one on the left has a halo round his head, and is Christ, or divine love; the other is blindfolded, and is Cupid, or human love. The object of the contest is to see which shall first pierce with his arrow a human heart, stuck on the top of a pointed pole, about five or six feet above their heads. The arrows, which are meant, according to the quotation from the Psalms, to be sharp,[1] are actually, by the way, blunter at the point than at the head. Cupid's arrow goes altogether askew, and misses the heart by a good foot. Christ, though apparently he aims no better, is successful in bringing the heart down. His success is sufficiently curious; for even supposing his arrow could, by a somersault, have hit the heart in falling (it falls, though not shot vertically,

---

[1] 'Sagittæ Potentis acutæ.'

in a line *parallel* to its first flight), a miracle
were needed (and is evidently wrought) to avoid
either driving the heart deeper on the pole, which
is far sharper than the arrow itself, or simply tear-
ing a bit out of it.   However, heart and arrow
come down safe and sound, within reach of his
hands.

In emblem 5 we are shown the dangers of
loving gold and silver and jewels.   The French
quotation is :—

> ' Le diable estrangle d'un noeud d'or
> Les Idolatres du Thresor.'

(The devil, with golden noose, strangles the idola-
ters of treasure.)   And the Latin tells us that ' those
who would become rich fall into temptation and
into the devil's noose.'   To exemplify this we see
a kneeling woman, who is gloating over an open
casket filled with chains, rings, and jewels.   One
big ornament she holds in her left hand, while
she plunges her right into a bag brimful of coins.
On a little rock, rising to the level of her neck,
stands the devil (with pointed beard, black eyes,
upturned moustache, horns, and a crown), holding
lightly in his right hand the end of a rope, which
has been passed in a slip-knot round her neck.
The long nails of his fingers are apparent, while
those of one foot are carefully displayed, just over
the edge of the rock he stands on.   He points to
the rope with his sceptre.

One of the prettiest pictures in its general effect is that representing the tyranny of worldly love (No. 6). Venus stands in a dainty little four-wheeled carriage and, with Cupid as her charioteer, is dragged along by her votary. This votary is again in a woman's form, and is attached by ropes round her neck to the front of the carriage, which is in the shape of a dragon's head. Cupid whips her on with his bow and bow-string. In this picture again there are curious slips in the drawing. To begin with, Venus's leg is too thick ; so are Cupid's legs. Then the off-wheels are, beyond the requirements of perspective, smaller than those on the near side. It is perhaps as well that Venus is standing, for the seat is at the back of the car behind the wheels, and if she sat down she and the car and Cupid would probably at once topple over backwards. On the other hand the car is charming in its design and orna-ment, and the fall of the drapery (that of Venus in particular) and its shading, may well afford some incidental ' douceur et contentement ' to him who is studying from the book ' les effects divers de l'amour divin et humain.'

The other pictures must be passed by, though one is tempted to linger over No. 11, where Absalom—with a happy simper—hangs by his hair in a quite inoffensive tree, transfixed by a tasselled spear, while a little Christ moralises to his pupil down below, ' Per quae quis peccat, per

THE TYRANNY OF EARTHLY LOVE
FROM M. VAN LOCHOM'S 'AMORIS DIVINI ET
HUMANI ANTIPATHIA'

ABSALOM

FROM M. VAN LOCHOM'S 'AMORIS DIVINI
ET HUMANI ANTIPATHIA'

haec et torquetur.' (A man is tormented in those things wherein he offends.)

Sufficient, however, has been said to show what are Lochom's methods in urging the choice of divine love rather than of earthly, and of showing the beguilements and stratagems of mundane desires.

The book affords an interesting sidelight on the state of mind of those to whom it appealed— a sidelight which, in my own particular copy, becomes oddly definite through a little poetical effort of one of its earlier owners. Inspired by these lines :—

> ' Quand la splendeur de la vermeille Aurore,
> Et le Soleil qui luy succede, & dore
> Tout l'uniuers . . .'

he blossoms forth thus, writing his verse on the back of emblem 31 :—

> ' When splendid Aurora rises from her Couch,
> Soon appears the Sun's reviving Beams; [*sic*]
> And thousand flowrets open to the Gleam.'

Let us hope, however, that but few of the owners were so like a Silas Wegg turned pious.

Inside the cover are the rhyming words— ' H. P. tenet me.' ' H. P.'—to judge from the book-plate immediately below it—was Henry Peckitt, M.A. He belonged, I have been told by my late friend Mr. J. V. Gregory, to a Thirsk family, and flourished about the beginning of the

last century.  The book-plate itself is on white
paper with the name engraved below.  I have
also an impression on green paper, and without
the name, in another of my little books.[1]

Four years later than this book of Lochom's,
namely in 1632, there was issued at Cologne the
third edition of Drexel's *Christian Zodiac, or the
Twelve Signs of Divine Predestination*; and this
little book stands on my shelf beside the other.
'Take this mirror,' says Drexel, speaking of his
book to the reader, 'and look into it each day.
Here you shall consider how many signs of predestination you find in yourself; whether all, or
none; one, or a few.   Hence, therefore, you shall
easily gather in which Book, that of Life or that
of Death, your name is written.   On the last day
of the world these Books, which are now closed,
shall be opened.   And he whose name is not
found written in the Book of Life shall be sent
into the lake of fire.   But they whose names are
written in heaven shall be filled with a deep and
everlasting joy.'
Well, these be great questions to settle out of
a little book, even though in its third and corrected edition.   Presumably Drexel thought the
earlier editions not quite safe in their guidance;
for he asks his readers to 'throw away that earlier

[1] The British Museum catalogue of the Franks Collection of Book-
Plates, by the way, speaks of yet another style—on brown-tinted paper.

*Zodiac* and take this, which is fuller and more correct, in its place!' Later in the book, indeed (in the 'Coronis, De paucitate prædestinatorum '), he speaks with less assurance as to conclusions whether men's names are in the one book or the other; quoting St. Bernard, that 'the Lord understands who are his own, and he alone knows whom he has chosen from the beginning. But of men, who knows if he be worthy of love or of hate?' Leaving aside, however, the question whether the third edition is finally trustworthy (I observe that there is certainly one other recorded!), let us consider instead what were the methods Drexel employed in his teaching.

The book consists of twelve sermons expounding the twelve emblems, and of a final sermon on the text, 'How few are they who are chosen!' ('De paucitate prædestinatorum.') It is in Latin throughout. Its engraved title-page reads as follows : 'Zodiacus | Christianus | locupletatus | Seu | Signa XII. Divinæ | Prædestina | tionis | Totidem Symbolis | explicata | Ab | Hierem : Drexelio | è Societate Jesu | [device] | Col : Agrippinæ | Apud Cornel : ab Egmond. | cIɔ.Iɔc.xxxii.'

The pictures that frame this title are charmingly and delicately executed, and include a Christ (at the top) sitting on a globe among the clouds, with brilliant radiance behind him, whilst a sword is near his left hand and a spray of a lily near his right. At the sides are two angels, with halos and wings, each holding before her, towards the reader, an open book. Below on the right is a sword, on the left a crown and sceptre, each outlined against a flame.

Turning now to the symbols themselves, the first is a candlestick with a burning wax candle. Its shadow (even, by the way, the shadow of the flame itself) is seen cast by some brighter light against the wall. This symbol is for ' lux interna,' and the verse ' Thy word is a lamp unto my feet, and a light unto my path,' is subjoined in Latin. It is, following the Latin Vulgate, assigned to Psalm cxviii. Then comes a sermon of seven pages.

The second symbol is a skull. Its drawing is the strongest in the book, and the mystery of its great dark cavities will linger in the memory. The inscription above it is ' Promptitudo ad mortem,' and Drexel's treatment of this subject will serve to illustrate the vigorous style which in his day made him famous as a preacher. If in places we find him something diffuse and ornate, we shall recall the more readily that he first made his mark as a student of rhetoric. Here, then, is an extract :—

' He who has lived well cannot die ill, nor can he die well who has lived ill. And what is this thing whose snatching away from us we so dread ? What is life but a stage filled with mockeries, a sea of troubles ? Wherever you sail in a ship, be it of

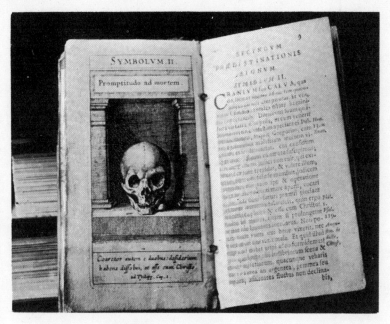

FROM DREXEL'S 'ZODIACUS CHRISTIANUS'

gold or of silver, of precious stones or of wood, you cannot evade the upleaping waves, you will often drive on to the rocks over against you, you will many a time stick fast in dangerous shallows. Blessed is he who has crossed this sea, blessed is he who has swum forth from it, and is already in the harbour. And if any one attain death ere his years are grown over-ripe, he should be no more grieved for than one who has made a swift voyage. Why then should we fear death, which is the end of toil and the beginning of our reward? It is the Lord's decree upon all flesh. In former ages none has escaped it, nor will any in future ages. How many soever have gone before, still all shall follow. To this law we are born, and whither all go, we also go. Death is the end for all, for many it is a remedy, for the upright it is even the heart's desire—assuredly so for those who are predestined to Life. For the troubles of all men alike Death is the solution and the limit, beyond which their ills do not pass. It were madness to withstand the decree of our blest Lord, and seek to compass a liberty which is granted to none. The faith of Christians is loftier, a faith which, taking life with patience, can yet long for death. The swan, if we believe Solinus, laments and grieves during life, but at death exults and sings. Likewise the elect groan whilst they live, but sing at the time of death, for they shall rejoice everlastingly in heaven. . . . Who would not rise quickly up from a hard couch? Those only linger who have made much of themselves in a warm bed of feathers, and can hardly leave that cosy nest. Does this life deal hardly with you? You will surely not grieve, then, to pass to a better. Is it well with you? Therefore the time is ripe for you to make an end speedily, lest prosperity should hurl you, like many another, into a tardy yet headlong ruin. Wherefore, says Tertullian, we should not fear that which frees us from all fear. God spares a man long torment when he grants him brief life. . . .

'Ambrose wondered that some men when they have to die would rather be thrust forth from their dungeon than led forth.

'"What is there," says he, "in this world and in this life except fighting against anger, lust, and gluttony?"

'Chrysostom is of the same mind. "What," he asks, "do you say, O man? You are called to a kingdom, even the Kingdom of the Son of God, and you stay there a mass of yawns, scratching yourself and sluggishly dozing!"'

The third symbol is again a striking one, and is of charming workmanship. The cup of the sacrament is standing on an altar. From out of the cup, and spreading above its rim, rises a circle of dazzling light, within which, on a shaded background, a crucifix is dimly figured. From the circle the light spreads in brilliant radiation,

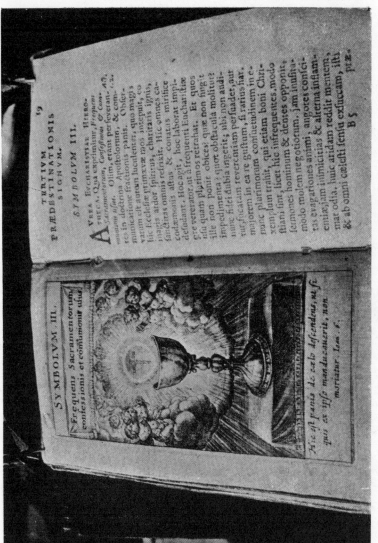

FROM DREXEL'S 'ZODIACUS CHRISTIANUS'

illuminating a throng of little angels and cherubs and the billowy clouds on which they rest. The angels are kneeling and holding out reverent clasped hands towards the Eucharist.

The fourth emblem is to symbolise the renunciation of all things, and bears beneath it the verse from the Epistle to the Philippians iii. 7 : 'Quae mihi fuerunt lucra, haec arbitratus sum propter Christum detrimenta.' (What things were gain to me, those I counted loss for Christ.) With true insight and restraint the artist shows nothing but a simple, empty altar.

It would be long to describe in detail all the illustrations, and indeed we should hardly be repaid for our trouble, for their value is unequal. Their subjects, however, may be briefly stated. The fifth is a rose-bush with many thorns, symbolising Perpetual Tribulation borne with patience; it has the text subjoined, 'Beati qui nunc fletis, quia ridebitis.' (Blessed are ye that weep now, for ye shall laugh.) The sixth is a fig-tree, and is made to represent the hearing of the Word of God. The seventh is a tobacco-plant, and is to figure alms given with kind feelings. The eighth is a cypress-tree, symbolising a humble opinion of oneself. The ninth represents love of enemies, and consists of two halberds (*hastae*, Lochom calls them) bound together by an olive garland.

This sermon, by the way, runs to twenty-three

pages, and includes quotations from Plautus and Aristotle, as well as from the usual religious sources.

In the tenth symbol a scourge and a bundle of rods (signifying detestation of former sins) hang from the arms of a cross. In the eleventh, an anchor is made to represent a proneness of the will towards what is good. The twelfth, and last, is a mandora (*cithara*, as the Latin says), by which is expressed control of the passions, or victory over temptation.

But if we pass by these emblems with brief notice, there is yet in almost all something good —whether a landscape in the background or some interesting symbolic idea. One would gladly know what the artist's name was ; whether it was that Raphael Sadeler who flourished about this time, and illustrated some part at least of Drexel's works in conjunction with other engravers. The book received its *imprimatur* in 1621 from Christopher Grenzing, when Sadeler was sixty-six years old and Drexel forty. This third edition therefore (1632) was the work of ripe years, being issued when Drexel was fifty-one.

My copy of the book, about the middle of last century, fell into the hands of a certain John Towneley, who put his book-plate into it. The plate is in the Chippendale style, and bears the motto ' Tenes le vraye.' John Towneley belonged to a second branch of the family,[1] as is shown by

---

[1] My informant was again Mr. Gregory.

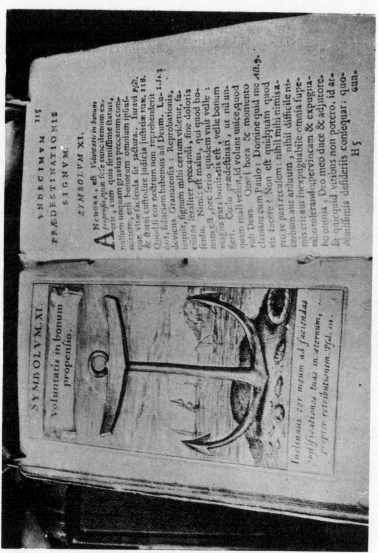

FROM DREXEL'S 'ZODIACUS CHRISTIANUS'

the crescent in the centre of the plate, and was one of the Towneleys of Towneley in Lancashire, who now hold some property in Stella, County Durham.

Nowadays, perhaps, comparatively few people would buy this book simply with a view to knowing whether they are predestined to bliss or torment, especially as it is written in Low Latin. Yet not a few would desire it (as in the first instance I did) for the sake of its illustrations; whilst some would want it for the sake of the book-plate. (As one friend said—'That is worth far more than the book itself!') Others, however, would be still interested in Drexel's forcible style, and his picturesque statement of religious truths. It is pleasant, too, to notice the range of his reading. He was, as his innumerable quotations show, deeply versed in the Fathers, and he quotes from, or refers to, the Classics with fair frequency. The Scriptures, of course, he knew thoroughly; he must have known familiarly too, one would judge, the *De Imitatione*, and the *Meditations* of Marcus Aurelius.

Such, then, are perhaps the things that at present chiefly interest us in Drexel and his *Christian Zodiac*, and that go to make up, for us, the significant quality of the volume. With Drexel's book, as with Lochom's, it is less the avowed intention of the work that is prized than the side interests and the incidental charm.

G

## IX

## SIXTEENTH-CENTURY DIALOGUES:
## A BOOK FOR TRAVELLERS

'How great is the usefulness of this little book
he will readily judge who either enjoys a knowledge of various tongues, or who has undertaken
a journey through different regions of our earth.
And while I think there is no one so dull of wit
as not to know its serviceableness, I think also
that there are many who kiss it heartily, and who
read it and handle it both day and night. Now
if, as is often done, parents send their children
abroad so as to further their studies, to form
their character, or to master foreign idioms, think
what will assuredly be said of the usefulness, nay
the necessity, of this book, since it affords, even
within one's own walls, a full and perfect knowledge of various languages in their everyday
experience. The day itself would run out were I
to try to recount its pleasantness, its beauty, its
excellence, and its other rich endowments.'

Curiosity is excited when one lights, in a
book-hunting ramble, on a little vellum-covered

volume whose Latin preface begins in this fashion. Its naïve complacency captivates us. We pay the few pence asked for it, tie the old green tapes with which it is fastened (and this must be done carefully, since they are rotten with age), and carry it home for more leisurely enjoyment.

The title-page is in three languages—Latin, French, and Flemish. The Latin simply says that the work consists of 'Dialogues and a small Dictionary in seven Languages—Flemish, English, German, Latin, Italian, Spanish, and French —a Book very necessary to all who are studying Languages at home or abroad.' The French, with a little more fullness, tells us that it has been revised, corrected, and enlarged, and that the dialogues are 'tres profitables et utils, tant au faict de marchandise, qu'aux voiages et aultres traffiques.' And the Flemish is to the same effect. The book was printed in the Netherlands, at Liège, and is a later edition of a work issued for the first time, apparently, in 1584.

It opens with a Latin poem of thirty-four hexameter lines, addressed by the Book to its Purchasers, in which promise is made, even if we stay at home, to instruct us in seven tongues, to the amazement of foreigners (this was perhaps realised, in a sense not quite intended), and we are intreated, if we must needs go abroad, at least to carry it with us, whether we are travelling

in the mighty realms of Spain, or are visiting the
'ever restless Frenchmen—

numquamve quietos
Francigenas.'

(The author himself is, we infer later on, a staid
Fleming.) Next comes the Latin preface, of
which we have already translated a portion ; and
thereafter, in full seven-tongued chorus, a fresh
introduction showing the scope and great merits
of the work. We will give the English portion
of this in full, first premising that if we silently
set right many of the misprints—*d*'s written as
*p*'s, *i*'s as *t*'s, words run together which should be
separate, the final letters of one word attached as
a prefix to the next word, and so forth—we do it
out of consideration for those readers who do not
possess the book, and who cannot, by referring to
the other tongues, find clues to guide them
through the obscurities. Further, we will write
modern *w*'s, and turn consonantal *u*'s into *v*'s ;
*e.g.*, we will write ' have,' not ' haue,' and ' flower,'
not ' flovver.'

To our Introduction, then : ' Beloved Reader,
this boocke is so need full and profitable, and the
usance of the same so necessarie, that his goodnes
even of learned men, is not fullie to be praised
for ther is noman in France, nor in this Nether-
land, nor in Spayne, or in Italie, handling [*i.e.*
trading] in these Netherlandes, which hat not

neede of these seven speaches that here in are writen and declared : fer whether that any man doo marchandise, or that hee do handle in the Court, or that hee followe the wartes [meaning ' warres'], or that hee be a travailling man, hy should neede to have an interpretour, for som of theese seven speaches. the which wee considering, have at our great cost, and to your great profite. brought the same speaches heere in suchwise together, and set them in order, so that you fromhence fouath [we leave philologists to settle in which dialects ' forth ' is pronounced ' fouath '] shal not neede any interpretour, but shalbe able to speake them your self, and to healp you ther with, and to know the maner of pronouncing of many nations. Wo [meaning ' who,' according to the other ' speaches'] hath ever ben able to set with one speach the frindship of sundry nations ? How many are ther becom ryche without the knowledg of divres languages? who can wel rule Landes and Cities, knowing none other lāguage then his mother tong onlie? whilst now it is thue ['thus,' friend Fleming!], beloved Reader, so receave this booke gladlie, through the which you may have the knowledg of seven divers languages : the which if you reade it with understanding and diligence, you shal finde that it shall be not onlie profitable for you, but also very needfull. And if so be that you may not learne the whole wit hout booke ['learn the whole by heart,' as we should say now; for the French runs, 'Que s'il ne vous vient à point de l'apprendre tout par cœur . . .'], then take out the same that you have most need of : This dooing you may whit pleasure, and in maner of speaking, all paying [*read* 'playing'; in the French column, 'en iouant'] com to the knowledg of many speaches or languages. Take therfore in good worth this our labou, thee which wee have don to your honour and profit. promising you that in case we finde the same by you to be wel accepted wee will at all times doo our diligence for to further you in thesame.'

After this, which is the third of the four introductory preliminaries, we come to the 'Table of this booke.' We once more hear that it is 'very profitable,' and learn that 'the first Chapter is a dynner of ten persons, and conteineth many common speaches which are used at te table.'

Having gained some insight into the less usually recognised 'beauties, excellencies, and other rich endowments' of English style and orthography in the sixteenth century, we shall now, in this 'dynner of ten persons' get a glimpse into the social life of the time. The scene is a Flemish one, though we have it in an English guise, and the appetites also are Flemish. After a little manœuvring and difficulty the guests (several of whom, by the way, are of the host's family) are got to their places. John is then told

to go fetch potage for his brother, and to runne
apace.  On bringing it he says : 'Brother, take
your potage, have you to much?'  Francis
answers : 'Iea, I have to much.'  John replies :
'Eatte it not all, let that alone which iee shall
have to much.'  Then Peter, the father (evidently
a thirsty soul), says : 'Give mee the biere pot.'
But his wife Marie answers : 'Peter, drinke not
after your potage, for it is unholsam : eate first a
little, before you drinke.  Peter cut me fleash,
cut mee also bread.  Cut Francis to eate, he hath
nothing to eate.'  Friend Peter, however, perhaps
a little sore about the 'biere pot,' answers : 'Must
I serve him?  Can hee not serve himself?  Cut
your self, you be great enough, help your self for
I wil not serv you : I serve no bodye, but mi
self.'  Soon Marie sends John to 'looke if the
pastyes and the tartes be brought.  Go fetch the
rostmeate, and fill heere wyne : fill for your
father, fill it full : fill nit so full. see you not
what you doe? you shead!'  (This last is not
an abusive epithet.  It only means 'you are
*shedding*, or spilling, it.')
    Then follows a procession of dishes—'shoulder
of meat, radishes, carrets, capers, hare, connyes,
patriches'—till we are not surprised to hear from
John that 'Ther is heere no mere [*i.e.* more]
Wine.'  He is, therefore, sent by his father to
fetch some 'theare as you fetched this. or go
fetchit on the market, at the white flower de lise

[*i.e.* the 'Fleur de Lis Blanche' inn] or whre you wil.' He is to get two quartes or three pintes, and is to 'go apace and com quicklie againe.' Exit John, promising to run all the way. Meanwhile, Francis is deputed to wait at table, after first being asked by Marie, 'Will you yeat have more meate? Speake boldlie.' To which he answers : 'No mother, I have eaten enough God be praysed.' Soon John returns with the wine. His thirsty parent at once asks him, 'How cometh it that you tarry so long?' but, with a view to getting to business, readily accepts his excuse 'I could not com sooner father. ther was many folckes. I have runne all the way,' and says : 'Well, fill heere wine.' The festivities still proceed. Soon we hear from Marie (they were valiant trenchermen in those days!) 'it is enough of drinking, we must eate also, I have great hunger: cut me there a peace of fleash.' Anne replies, with what may seem scant courtesy, 'Have you no handes?' Marie explains : 'Yes, but I can not wel reach tho ['to'] the platter.' Then paterfamilias breaks in : 'Well, I will serve you : have you enough?' *Marie* : 'I have yet nothing.' *Peter* : 'Holde there, have you enough now?' *Marie* : 'Looke what hee geeveth me ; keepe it for you, and eate it your self. Roger, cut me of that shoulder.' We hear, in due course, of 'cleane trenchers, freutte and cheese,' and when these have been disposed of, the talk at last becomes a little more general; for a few minutes questions of eating are left aside, while the chances of the war ending and peace being established are discussed. Then, when grace has been said, friend Peter characteristically suggests : 'Let us drinke after the grace.' Roger seconds him : 'That it is well saide,' and adds : 'Peter, how much wine have wee had? We will pay for the wine.' *Peter* : 'Yee shal not truble, yee shall geve nothing, once for al : if I have had the power to give you to eate, I shall have it also to give you to drinke.' *Roger* : 'What should that be? The wine is now deere.' *Peter* : 'Yee heare what I saye.' *David* : 'Well then we thanke you, we must deserve it.' *Marie* : 'It is all deserved.' *Peter* : 'I thank you also, that yee are com.' Soon after these bland courtesies have been interchanged, they find that it is ten o'clock, and so is time to separate. John is sent to fetch the lantern, and the party breaks up.

The scene to which we are next introduced by our versatile guide and instructor is quite different in character. He is now minded that we should 'learne to buye and sell,' and therefore takes us one chilly morning into the streets and market - place, where, wandering among the booths and shops, we may master the intricacies of the cheapening art. A chapwoman, by name Margaret, is waiting at one of the doors, on the look-out for customers. To her enter Katharin, who greets her : 'God geeve you god morrow gossip, and your company.' Margaret answers : 'And you also gossip.' *Katharin* : 'What do you heere so earlie in the coulde? have you ben heere long ?' *Margaret* : 'About an hower.' *Katharin* : 'Have you solde much to daye ?' *Margaret* : 'What sholde I have aredy solde? I have not yeat taken handsaile.' *Katharin* : 'Nether yet I.' *Margaret* : 'Be of good chere, it is yeat earlie : God wil send us som marchantes.' *Katharin* : 'I hope so : heere cometh one, hee wil com hether. Frinde, what wil you bue? Com hether, pleaseth it you to buye any thing? looke if i have nothing that lyket you. Com in, I have heere good cloth, good linen cloth, of all sortes : good silke, chamlet, damaske, velvet : I have also good fleash, good fish, and good herringes. Heere is good butter, and good keese also, of all sortes. Will you buye a goed cap? or a good booke in French? or in Duth ? or in Latin ? or a wirting book [*i.e.* 'writing book']. Buye som what : looke wat pleaset you to buye, I will sell it you good cheape, aske for what pleaset you, I wil let you see it, the sight shall cost you nothing.' The customer, David, thus introduced to Katharin's motley collection (notice, by the way, how completely Katharin has 'cut out' her gossip Margaret, carrying off the prey to her own general store), asks a few random questions about some of the articles exposed for sale, and then sets to serious bargaining over a piece of cloth. Katharin asks for it 'seventeene stuvers and a half.' David says he 'wil geeve therfore twelve stuvers' only. They haggle on for some time without result; no bargain seems to be possible. So Katharin says: 'Wel, God guyde you: go looke somwere els, if you can buye better cheape; you shall have it no wheare for less price: I am able to sell it you as good cheape as another, but I wil not leese therby: I let you have it almost for that price that it cost mee: I must winne som what, I sit not heere to winne nothing, I must lieve therby.' And so on through the shifts of feminine ingenuity! At last a middle price is struck, and after a final skirmish about the 'change' out of the coin he tenders (for she professes 'I have no smal mony') matters are adjusted, and they then start bargaining about other articles.

But it is time that this sketch drew to a conclusion. We would gladly linger for a little over Chapter IV., in which two friends are riding, on a summer's evening, into Antwerp. The laments of one over 'the dust that doth put out me eyes,' and the ready resource of the other, who bids him 'take this taffeta to put before your face, and it will keepe you from the dust and from the sunne'; the method of asking the way of a 'shee sheapherd' whom they luckily meet: 'My shee freend, where is the right way

from hence to Antwerp?'; their fears of 'theeves':
'they did rob thoter day a riche marchant hart
by this tree';—all this is quaintly entertaining.
But we must leave further investigation to the
curious, commending to their notice more especially the scene in the inn at night.  Here they
will watch with amusement the illness (is it
wholly or only partly feigned?) of one of the
guests who is anxious to get away and have a
few minutes of quiet flirtation with the maid
Joan.  She sees through him, however, in spite
of his pathetic assurance that 'I sheake as a
leafe: upon thee tree'; for when he presently
says: 'My shee frinde, kisse me once: and I
shall sleape the better,' she replies: 'Sleape,
sleape, you are not sicke seeing that you speake
of kissyng,' and so exit.

We may add that the author was not altogether
wrong in predicting some celebrity for his book,
since it ran through twelve or thirteen editions
within eighty years.  The little volume evidently
managed to supply what was 'a long felt need'
to a bygone generation.

THE OLD BOOKMAN'S RETREAT.

FROM A DRAWING BY MARGARET ANDERTON, R.D.S.

## X

# THE OLD BOOKMAN'S RETREAT

WHEN he is grown old, and bread-winning is become a weariness to him, our bookman, if he have but enough savings, will journey to a sunny place he wots of, where a little town is perched high above the world on the top of a steep hill. There is a citadel in it for safety, a cathedral for beauty, and a library for delight. In some tranquil Rue des Echos, where the world's din and vexations shall be but as memories to him, or as a half-heard rumour, he will live out the quiet remnant of his days. He will bask in the hot sunshine, will walk at his ease under long avenues of elm-trees, sit at the foot of cool grey ramparts overlooking the long levels of the fields beneath, and anon, at home among his books, will pore over the old volumes, gathering up the threads of thought which, in a life filled with diverse occupation, had remained disunited and elusive. Perchance, too, using such art of style as is within his faculty, he will himself add a little to the melody of life by writing upon the things that are a joy to him: his long fidelity to books will have brought him discernment and a not trivial sense of beauty.

In such pursuits will the evening of his life be spent—an evening luminous and calm, not lacking its sunset radiance.

## NOTE TO CONCORDIO

### (*Page* 33.)

*It may be mentioned that this is not a mere imaginary study, but is a record of my own early music master, J. F. Borschitzky—'Mr. Bor,' as we used to call him. I would gladly, if it might be, keep his memory just a little longer from the 'waters of oblivion.'*

B. A.